We Step into the Sea

New and Selected Poems

To the possible world

Contents

Part 1—A Garland

What Is God in Us

On a hill
In the rain
Just the same
I am crawling
Toward you
You are the last
Site of our second
Now I am rising
Three now in you

Three Now in You: A Creation Myth

I turned to the children and to you
And could not see your faces
       A shadow-I had crept from me
She gazed now at all
       The vast human races
Sitting down beneath
       A desert-willow tree
Shadow-I absorbed every hue
       There white had shed its mystery
A 19th century's journey's end
       Total eclipse of Gordon Pym
Disarmed the policemen
       Looking down from a hill
With miracle power and mystic skill
       No hue no shape no sex
Picked out for first disgrace
       Shadow-I saw the human races
Walk away from original skin
       Into a day not yet named

Into a Day Not Yet Named

Consider the painted flower

Toiling not

In sheer blue and yellow

Peach and Plum

A pair of happy dogs

O sweet meantime

Pointillist of presence

The baby cradles mother

In black and white

Before color was an option

An angel dreamed you

An Angel Dreamed You

The poet came by sailboat
She was salty
A pirate Paraclete
A sky holy and wholly
One shoulder slightly bared
In the great big har-har

Fish wooed her   One in particular
Was it a fish or an angel
In the great big won't-you-be-mine
It was an angelfish
She was a poet
We were their marriage poem

We Were Their Marriage Poem

Many of us wept at the funeral
You were in the casket and so was she
By now We were a dearth
Seen from above in the aerial photograph

By now Us was a Them
I saw everywhere
Are you Them?
Is she? And where does you stand?

I was crying in the rain at the funeral
Many of Them wept too for the dream
Is there a pattern to our grief?
A chalk trace for our Body?

Crying in the rain at the funeral
Heart-shaped tears maudlin ovals
Streams of affection lost

By now Us was a refrain
Buried beside Them in the box
Where bit by bit
The sorrows of separation were shifted

The Sorrows of Separation Were Shifted

"We" had become unreal
Feathers of an extinct bird
Glued to library shelves
And nothing worth reading there

We divorced on Facebook
Shared the children's status
They were healthy   happy
Now they had become genre

Social in our surveillance
The difference multiplies
Though the record shows
Friends in the thousands

Glee was a TV show
Not available on our plan
Allegory had returned

She was still a girl
Her name was Rape

Her Name Was Rape

Principle   is only found alone

Gandhi, for example   A calf was maimed   An animal

Suffered without cause   & so was killed

In *Ahimsa* "as with one so with all"

A concept of love   A slavery

John Brown, for example   as with one so with all

& His sons murdering for him   too are murdered

A concept of love   Gandhi:

"Suppose, for instance, that I find my daughter—whose wish at the moment I have no means of ascertaining—is threatened with violation and there is no way I can save her, then it would be the purest form of *ahimsa* on my part to put an end to her life and surrender myself to the fury of the incensed ruffian."

Her wish: Muffled in a calf's dying bleat

My wish: To love

What is God in Us

Part 2—

"The covenant is
There shall be peoples"—George Oppen

Air Said Say It Again

Creature in each and each in oh
Seeds in our hair
Future child a smile
Beside a stair

Trio of origin
Sister left to father
To brother you

Ventricles of a single sound
Age goes behind Falls ahead
On the bulletin board of your choosing

A genius sits beneath her portrait
Christ has left the cross
A boy gets caught in the arms
Of his dead father's suit

Memory lost its smell
Blue ribbons   There were blue
Ribbons everywhere
Though first was clearly gone

Madonna in miniature
Talk about daily bread
Daily bread
Bulletin board

Life-Sentence(s)

One full-grown woman
A recently born child
A gleam of sunshine
& Pointed hill
One saint in a silent movie
Agee in a cab
Martin King on a Memphis balcony
Clouds when examined under glass
Salt water on solid rock
Jesus on the cross
Father in the guest room
4 to 6 feet
Now
Stupid Fucking White Man
Then
A pebble and a clod
The Future
Mr. William Blake
The stars of the southern hemisphere
Moisture
The climbing up
Doris Lanard
The climbing down

Robert Creeley

Overhanging ferns and lilies

A level and brilliantly white sea

A little haystack

Port Desire

The first landing

Flaccid Overlook

Entropy's missed triumph

Your luminous body

Mine

Are You Anyone

Are you anyone
Really are you someone
And which one do you think

Are you watching the water now
The water now falling
Upwards then down
From the fountain

You weren't watching only were you
You were listening too and which came first
When you saw that you saw
The water falling

Is anything really itself is it
I mean is that part
Of what she meant
What anyone meant
When looking they also heard

When I'm not anyone
Are you no one too

When we say we are we sure
There is agreement
Who are we
& whee, whee, whee
Where is home

The leaf takes the tree
But not me
Though they *blow blow blow*
At my feet

When they say we
There is no
No agreement
They're not we
And *whee whee whee*
We are home

The wind hits the pane
There is pain
Blown in the rafter
It looks like leaves

Could I be a leaf
Could I and what kind

Once I knew you were me
There was someone sweet in the sound

Mr. Birdsong lives down the lane
His house has fallen from the tree

When will he sing again
When will I free me

The Power and the Glory

My age liked its Mystery
Confined to Formula
Though I saw the Incarnation everywhere
The Risen Lord dead by knife on Street A
The Fictional Real crammed into a pothole
On Ramrod Avenue

The Holy itself chased by whole armies
Only to die unafraid before the Host
Of Loyalists tonguing categories
Like a salt lick   Baby roaches
   A bunch of baby roaches
Asleep on the side of a Kleenex box

Oboe Hymnal

I loved you

      You were an oboe

Singular and grave

The inside of my mouth

      Played you

We drove together
The earth was suffering

What was hurt wanted to shine
Sanctuary and true
Directly above the potholes

The truth is a pothole
And men are scraping there

Though you   my oboe
Replace them

I loved you

      You were an oboe
Tiptoeing careful and grave inside

"They fix things for us" Ben says
Bareheaded men looking down
So many versions of men looking down
Scraping us away from here

No mathematics!
Speaking now
To the inside of my mouth:

Rest

Speaking now to the fictional real:
I believe in you
Sanctuary and true
Shining directly above the pothole
And into the ruin where I find you

Though the ruin is not you
Curled   Proud   Your invisible shape your effort

Curled there almost comfortably
Between so many men looking down

Are they here for you too?

Why else are they striking the ground?

Oboe?

After a Lifetime Spent in Air

A deer tongues a salt lick
At the edge of my inner eye
Its almond-shaped eyes looking upward
A medieval saint insane thirst
Or both

From here it seems all right
The earth sloughing off its aborigines
Rolling faster to scratch the itch
Your round-faced little darling
One stage in a new epidemic

My neighbor is leaving her husband
Everything is always "going around"
I can't catch anything
White pines   thin ghosts in the dark
Find me   even in the desert
Living on the head of a pin

My informer indicated the similarities
Between ululating and elation
All lost to me
A wave   an ordinary undulation
Effecting the mainland
Until the sand is wiped clean

Poem with Some Words from Charles Ives' "The Majority," The Ghost of e.e. cummings Presiding

Hog-Mind thus created by

        & from the pursuit of h. and thus of a.

        and b.

Hmmed above the public terrace

        & grunted "mine"

The non-people inside the people strolling and dreaming

Non-people in the people hand in hand

Strolling beneath the Alhambra in radioactive sand

Brute Force built a power plane behind their houses

Thus energy was occupation

Hog-Mind summons his handmaidens

Non and the   open and closed   the many the few

His prurience a given   a true

The Slovenly Paradise

Beaucoup de petites fleurs
Little yellow weeds
Thriving in the nuclear sun

A bright light   A girl named Lucie
Pitching her tent indoors

Deprivation killed the honor students
Kneeling execution-style
Against the schoolyard wall

Labor hired the executioner
And freedom of speech
Is absorbed in holy robes

Maybe this really is paradise
And life proper is a weedy yard
And a girl serving tea under a sheet

May poetry let her stay there
An invisible campfire
The true God come down again

Circa 2016

John Clare eats grass and knows he is Childe Harold
Jane Bowles' small hand reaches across whole worlds to hold mine

I feel the desperate dead
Restlessly looking for lost worlds

97 years ago Las Vegas was wetland
A vast grazing plain for cattle and wild animals

Our migration will look different
Abandoning the city in our Taco Bell uniforms
We scavenge the desolate Cracker Barrels for food
Along Interstate 15

It Will Vanish

It will vanish
With the lizard
We will

The gauze-cut sky
And the unfolding generations

A child *en route*
His first tour of hatred

Ceaselessly loving
Disappearance cancels the tours
Vanishing will vanish my lizard

Had awakened wanting
To touch your face
You were not there
Though I called   I called
For you   your disappearing
Vanquishing vanishing

Dear lizard   You were everywhere

There were many eyes
Open in the gauze-cut sky

A child astride a lizard

En route the tour

Begins to vanish

Begins to vanish
Though I called I called
"Little lizard   no disappearing!"

"[Christel] is the only God—And so am I and so are you"
    —William Blake
"Split the stick and there is Jesus"—John Cage

Where would I put my body

If not with you

Where is the tree

If not in me

The shadow takes the wall

Blue mountains rise above our colorless

Our color free our color and need are free

Francis is my saint

Am I a bird on his shoulder

We have kept our broken toys

Dragonfly hovers through my kneeling

Sister Cypress brown

Dying from the top down

Brother ass in paradise

In London   In Assisi

            In the meadows

Our colorless our color free

Out need color and free

Sheep come lost

Sheep come lost in the found

Such nappy hair

Such earthy smell

Am I a bird in your mouth   Am I

Singing to sheep

Living in sheep   shaped in color

Neither needy   nor found

A Posy

Swells and swells and falls behind
Love came in kind so long a sound
A sound swells sweet so clear our eyes
Love came that way that way to wash
To swell behind to clear the eyes
The wall the walls we loved the walls
We loved the walls into a cry
A year a *yo* a year sweet treat
In heart in time the love in *kine*
Goes a good way for to *why*
A sound a climb *up up* it swells
It sways and weighs up from behind
Back song climes ahead ago
And *yo to* love and *yo* to love
No more *no no* to nay or no
The heart's bit string a sweet thread
A treat to hear to eat to clove
To bits the wall this *yo* a treat
To hear to eat the treat *ho ho*
Is love

Part 3—And rolled a great stone to the sepulcher, and departed.—*The Jefferson Bible*

Nature Propositions

1. Nature has no regard for humans

2. Or what humans call regard is lost in nature

3. Which moves forward regardless

4. "Living with regard for others she became unnatural"

5. It felt good

6. It felt bad

7. Nature moved forward regardless

8. They were in it together

9. Nature and the others

Dark Eulogy

Mother   your miners   suffocate miles inside you

      & Father   Always helpless sea god

You can't help your daughters escape their terrible deaths

Every century finds its method of tapping her

      I hear machines in the paradise

    & Calliope shrieking inside their whine

Mama has forgotten me

& still the children   mouths overfull with gods

Little Elegy for Bill Knott
His Words and Disaster Notes Presiding

The true orphan opts for vasectomy
"Heart...de facto amazon remained"
Plot genie *sans* child hidden or contained
What's not born is tenderness other lies

Outremer where God died lost in a sneeze
Deux ex machina first cyborg of all
Your desert honeymoon pinned to yon wall
Sifts in the vast Deferens cools the breeze

Les Differences mon ami bred hardpan
It was the only nation that remained
Mother-other sole partisan to blame
She's any woman you could ever name

"Stepped on...lost...lost as she is to me I
...[I] rather...under her be...than their eyes"

Bright Eulogy (Ferguson)

No mistakes in the mistake
Buddha inviolate in a leaf
Crosses of all material
Links beam to beam
A just addition

She's a friend in Jesus
Crucifixion all around
Here's real mission creep
Another's son dead for hours
Unburied on the ground

Pontius Policeman a stick figure
A clerk a weasel a pawn-filled god
Petals spill from our girl's mouth
In bright eulogy
Uplifting the dawn

Outside Story

A sheered cliff

The carpenter's son

(gone)

Water line splits light

Crossing desert shadow

Shaking branches

(Stop)

So many ugly sisters

At least two

Clawing the sacred outside

Got blood under the nail

Under the nail

The carpenter's son

(Gone)

Shaking tree

(Stop)

Ugly sisters hurt outside

Eyes close in her head

Nail me

Nail me sacred

(Scared)

Water line splits light

Shadow makes a cross

Aramaic cliffs

Which way to Mt. Olive

Ugly sister introduced nail

Got the poem here

No need to say get her out of here

Get her out of here

On your right/on your left

& Stealing

Invite her home

In the Primer of Primary Things

The inner life got left in the rain
Thereafter and further
She's called wet and Wet
She calls out your first name

Segundo Primer

She had molded   the hands and feet
On the sculptor's   famous statues
And stopped there

Led strangers   to the new world
And died there

She is sold now   in Las Vegas
There are many   versions of her
7, 12,   17 years old
Stolen from   every part
Of the   old world
Which has not died

She is the   remnant talking
          Remnant *spiritus mundi*
The glorious mathematic
Stalled   in proliferation

No more births!
She's smiling from   the side of her eyes
          Wet tears on your face

In the Primer of Material Things

So one just keeps going
      Without belief
With and without belief

The quality of the machine
A baggage truck at least
A ton and turning
With precision between
Two airplanes

But that is his world

The body of poetry
Compromised by talk
Year after year
Driven by talk

Afraid up there now
Of mind leaving

Though that transit is true
And nothing to do
With the odor of the university
The dry skin falling on a book
& Everyone pointing to collapse
Along with those who believe
That money is a kind of poetry

Eddie laughing in the rubble he loves
The pines hundreds of years old around him
Alice in disobedience on *Gare du Nord*

Brother   Sister

In their lives
                The body of poetry

A Shasta lily white and streaked by violet
Inhabited by a spider
White and streaked by violet

How to honor those forms of life
Embraced by exile and dispossession
Eddie's house collapsing around him
His septic field failed
Alice jogging to *l'hopital* in Paris
A Great American Poet moved away
To the cures offered free elsewhere

The Shasta lily closing
& A spider white
& Streaked with violet
Climbing down the stem

Samaritan Treatment

The feminine wager, by degrees, transforms boys to girls.

A king is a man not home at home.

He won't take the blame

For his home not home, the air's heavy ruin.

The feminine wager is aging.

On a world stage, she's wearing a crown

And the king is a series of cufflinks in a museum.

It's a civil rights museum and the cufflinks,

Particularly the pearl, set the stage for her disgrace.

She is wagered into a road,

The Jericho Road, a road for strangers.

A road where strangers via sisters,

Via brothers, arrive in others.

Her crown is rolling down the Jericho Road.

The king is weeping as he follows it.

The boy inside the girl smiles into his beard.

Never wager with care. Take care of care.

Her care wages statue, then pearl.

By degrees, cufflinks to handcuffs

Detain strangers on roads.

Brothers and sisters, poets all

Roll their others at a weeping king.

For Cuba

Beautiful island,
         Resist beyond my life.

My father's Chevy glides across you,
One of the simple machines
Built to outlast the world.

Make me a doorstop.
Fashion the day upon a seesaw.
History is a load tipped on one wheel,
Singing inside a barrel.

Cuba libre and somehow she is,
Her lilies purple and red,
A showy squill under pines.

Caribbean sister,
         My refugee drifts below deck.
A craft wed to music,
She's floating now
Toward something free.

Nutshell

Like a pine cone sitting on glass   Nature in time

      Hid in clear sight   Like an egg hovering over a nest

We were not home at home   Like the marble heart my son brought

      To hold down my papers   We were hard and not kind

Like the Holy Family in a nutshell   We looked in vain at the stars

      Like *like* itself   Our hope slipped slowly backward

I wanted to reach for   A little gratitude   But she divorced me

Leaving only responsibility, her stingy sister   She sat down so hard

"Like, *forever*"   On my heart   Like raking the sand

Like music left with only a drum   The clouds painted

Like the roadrunner the carnivore the real one   & not the cartoon

      Eating one by little one the baby quail

      All that's not ever again for dinner

The Suffering Lost Its Gaze

The suffering lost its gaze,
Since in time, time was a cage.
It was Friday, the young dead again
From The Age.

Neither Ishtar, nor Easter,
Pasque flower in sequester,
Where the old doctor glowers
Deep in a yellow glass.

Had seen the social fabric
Stretched sheer in cadaver.
We were a body,
Staking rest in a fester.

How it bloomed!
Bruise yellow and brown,
Our body tattooed
On first grounds:

Which is son, and our daughter,
At home in all hours,
Seeking station, and in station
Simply stayed .

Where to stay
Is not rest, but lifelong
Duress , what is true
Held down by a clamp.

On the chest, or the bone,
Where you awake, you alone
Saw the holy driven thin
In a hole.

The man there seems familiar.
They have killed all his sons,
And their corpses
Made the front page
Page lost now in time,
With the horses that are gone
And the words once print graze
In grass dark with foals.

Permanently Stranger

Not yet light   in Nevada Trails
     Dawn   Followed The tradition of dispossession
& I   sank   afloat in legacy

Boom or bust   day arrives gleeful on the tour bus
We drive through paint more azure than azure

This is different from exile
A form of private life   or a parking lot
A documentary dedicated to the root
-Lessness that comes   prior or adjacent

To revelation   which is only dust
Man-made *and* organic
Turning the sky such a magnificent red

I wouldn't be you   for anything
Or me for that matter
We don't want to end up   in the garage
     Filthy with all the other objects

Your 200-year-old house on the prairie
Sits on prairie dogs rife with bubonic plague

When a bus hits a postmodernist
     The bus dies

Getting Particular

"I am not important and I know it . . .

Now I'm important"

& The built-in contingency

That I might hurts You

As You did Me

But not I not You but how we're We

Messed up the living room;

& It is certainly my

"Female identity as awakened in

Intimacy with another"

Hinged to your "male identity, forged in relation to the world"

Hammer & anvil sunbeam sunbeam

The Whole's the question

So never worry those others beside You

Will get lost here

We is beyond Modern

We is Free

Oppen's Sailboat

Was not Mallarmé's
Though made of words
A chance glint
Of some mineral
Element however
American the space it took
To be there really

Not signing his name
He made it with his own hand

The sailboat is mine
If I write it

The planet is ours
People really say that

Ours sails inside hours

The word needed was Niedecker
Lorine   her knowing

When water makes a movement
The sailboat turns and there is meaning
A life and stars *étoiles*
As Mallarmé sets forth

Part 4:

We

Step

Into

The

Sea

"Now begins to rise in me the familiar rhythm; words that have lain dormant now lift, now toss their crests, and fall and rise, and falls again. I am a poet, yes. Surely I am a great poet."

–Virgina Woolf *from The Waves*

With a string of flowers   Around our neck

With our mouths overfull   Of our sisters in

A garland with bricks in dresses   In our leis

With our sea wreaths and   Our coronas

Wind blows across   Look there it's   A surface

Look lookout   Up periscope   Look a friend

Been a pair o ragged claws Oh   o more pa's church!

With sisters made stone   In bricks   In dresses drown

At sea I see   Gertrude Mina Adrienne Brenda & Alice

With a podium tied to my foot   & The kids keeping score

I say when it's all over poetry will live   Poetry is proof

Community it turns out   Is a garage sale   All your

Panties amid toys blow dryers   & mama's art dad' s brief

-Case our brother   a sweet child in a dusty photograph

Dressed up in short pants   & long coat Sister all Coco

Chanel on the front porch   With a serving tray made

From Monarch butterflies   *That* was my Argentina

That and a fuchsia Poncho   Where I let the boy in

We're a girl and a boy   Kissing in the poncho

In a   purple poncho   On the beach where

We're just becoming   &   That boy   he dies

Years later   He shoots himself   1 shot

1 shot   I'm in college   & in 2 more years

My 2 best friends' brothers   They too kill

Themselves But my brother My brother my bro

He dreams in prophecy/ & In parable: A lady

She's drowning   He sees   He sees long black hair

And a blue swimsuit   He sees through waves

Papa says "No one sees through waves"   It's breakfast

Orange juice & French toast   But Eddie dreaming gives

A hand She takes it He can't hold   She slips out of reach

He's asleep   It's a dream he tells in morning   & He goes

Running & She is dead on the sand She's ashore   O Miramar

O "Sea-sight" Here & now that Brother starts to drown   O

Miramar the sea in dreams each night   *Lulalulaylulalulaylu*

Lay It's dream science "extrasensory perception" ESP 6th

Sense prophecy in dreams   A telepathy Or precognition

In *gnosis* Eddie is dreaming   & 2 weeks later her boat

The *Carpe Diem*   We find ashore On Miramar beach

No fact got through known bodily sense   But felt

In clairvoyance dreams/telepathy   / Precognition

In *gnosis* Eddie couldn't   Just openly see it

Or hold/keep a finger/his hand   /To it   /To Her

Since he saw her death   Behind shut eyes

His sleep now death   Behind his shut-eyes

And in sleep's remnant   Dream is shed gone

By   O Seabirds they dive & Don't rise again

Eddie   You saw through the veil The sea's prow

Where   Our lady of the blue-bathing suit Passed

In what manner   But for sight Is the seer rewarded

O Mavis sing Mavis let's sing   Away inheritance

Sing through the pinhole   Fled through pinhole's Mavis

Miramar/is sea-sight /My only brother running/ his gaze

Ties foresight & the long-distance runner Sight's prophecy

Wherein the seabirds dive and never rise Steve   Mike Chris

All of us children find the boat ashore   It really was named

The *Carpe Diem* The *Carpe Diem* beached ashore   2 weeks

After 2 runners found her drowned Eddie & Bob found her

Lady in a blue swimsuit ashore & When the ranger says

"Just take her hand boys" Eddie re-members In dream

He reaches toward her Her hand   He can almost see

Through it They're transparent   Seeing through

Waves   He touches her hand Loses her   She slips

Away He wakes in the morning   There is orange

Juice and talking Dad says no   Says nobody

Nobody sees through waves   Says   Nobody

Can see through waves   Now a pinhole is

Opening   *Lulaylulaylulaylulaylulay* opens

The ocean is crashing   & Crashing & waves

Follow the other   Rising cresting & clanging

The foghorn's call in our ears at night a   Siren

It is the Sirens   We heard nights

There were many of them   I heard they were born

In rivers & they were longing for still water: "We

Won't discriminate   /She's a woman we love in boats

A-crashing/ or boys   Running or the girl/You asleep

In our Singing/Who is Listening   / girl-bird or (Mavis)?

We are mariners of your Sleep   We live in your dreams

We sing inside your breath   We followed your sister all

Coco Chanel on a front porch Holding a tray made fully

From Monarch butterflies There are photos of us at the

Garage sale by her panties near the toys & piñata   the

Toys and blow dryers   mama's art daddy's briefcase

Wearing the head of a bird-girl or legs of   a bird

We're in whatever case beautiful in *my* Argentina

Where we hold fuchsia in purple ponchos & fit

Between boy & girl heard a shot   so loud it

Kills him   We saw all vanish   We the lone

-Liest girl birds had forgiven   well even

Everybody's abandonment   O come here

I'm gazing up at you I'm youngest   My bro-

Ther early saw death &   Saw death had nothing

To do with prophecy and so   He stopped running

With a string of flowers round our necks   mouths

Overfull of sisters :   "We won't discriminate/ It's a

Woman we love in boats A-crashing/   or boys running

Or a girl/ You asleep In our Singing/   Who is Listening /

Girl-bird / or (Mavis)?   We are mariners of your sleep

We're alive inside your dreams /   We're singing inside your

Breath   We followed sister all Coco Chanel on the front

Porch holding a tray made entirely from butterflies   There

Were pictures of us at the sale by panties near toys   near

Piñatas toys blow-dryers mama's art   daddy's briefcase

We're wearing heads of a bird-girl   We're in whatever

Case beautiful in *my* Argentina where we fit fuchsia

In purple ponchos O Mavis sing Mavis   Let's sing

Through the pinhole in a garland in a brick-dress

In our leis with no more than a   sea wreath &

Our coronas   & flowers around   our necks

Look lookout up periscope   Look   a friend

Such Little Things

I miss the mark   draw bow & try again

Am not conscious of hating   God or Us   right or love

I have swum   all my days   a little cold

There is none but honey sweetness such little things

The world placed in me

from *Refinery* 1994

No Excuses

The grass is wild.
It starts like that.
The teeth and the meadow
of hair at your neck and then:
the gun is wild.

       The coyotes trailed
The long tractor mowing the hay for winter.
The blades churned the field mice up in its wake,
into the mouths of the waiting dogs. The blades were the sun
for both planets, *mouse* and *dog*.

This story is not mine and the sun reflected
on the clay road there is wild. The tree thickets
are wild. The sun in the blades of grass
in the meadow is not mine but see how I live in the air,
all three—*tractor, mice, hungry dogs*—travel, doing
my job, tearing through notions of grass
and flesh to make sense of the embarrassing,
unrestrained sky. The sun pours down like rain

on the wild underbrush near the edge
of Remorse, the closest town,
where the deputy has just killed
the innocent fugitive with one shot.
His dull slug jails me in the barred backseat
of the present: almost servile, this contrived
instinct gulps water sniffed out by my dearest
enemy: I lie down and reason rifles my hair.

Sanctuary

Miss World of 1939 is sad.
Alone in her art gallery
circa 1980, the winged
Indian man of god burns
fluorescently in her honor.
Who will dare to let her make her bed?
The grey in her eyes curves
away from possession, living
somewhere so humid and dense,
those who left when she was
crowned have been years, and still
not found her, in the travel.
I want to protect Miss World,
take her away from these carnival
crucifixes, free her from yet
another grinning Nazi dinner
party, forever. Of herself
she says only, "I knew, you see,
there was a needle in the skin
between my thumb and index
but I could not, no I
refused to open my eyes.
The doctor kept asking,
Are you angry, are you angry,
but I had named that needle before
with my eyes closed." Her hands folded
into a temple in her lap. "You will
never know how sad." How many, dear
beauty, how many longed to crawl
to safety under those hands? Relics,
Miss World, in hissing human form,
of what we'd do to own you.

Romanticism

It is not the clay road
on which a woman travels
clutching a baby in one arm
and holding an older boy's hand
while he eats an apple.
I think it must be
in what the boy sees as he walks
there, caught in the sweetness
of apple, in the love it allows
him as he bites suddenly
his cheek, as he turns his face
up to his mother, wanting to cry
but stopping himself, *How tired
she is*, and he has only just begun
to bleed. And it's how I want
to let him keep looking away
from her who has his hand,
at wildflowers, the old town,
anywhere but at his feet.

Where the Train Meets the River

Believe me, I wanted
        the reply my life
couldn't smear the tracings
        of in the rain's low-
voweled madness against the train
        window. I was falling
in that reflected downpour, trees' arms
        skeletal in the excess space
the sky fakes, my twice-removed blood,
        my parenthetical bond,
finally only the sudden catch the Charles River
        gleaned in my throat
after the darkness of the tunnel. Only a moment,
        only a moment was my life
removed from the face I looked away from
        in the window. I wanted to be on
the train. I wanted to be more than reflection.
        I wanted to put my fingers
into the mouth of the baby's scream ricocheting
        in the suddenly quiet car,
but the gathering roar works as a buffer
        to infant trauma as if anything
so loud, so deafening, must be god,
        so instinctively baby stops
to listen. It's mother's *shh, shh* taking form
        in the train's gaining momentum,
the whispered lullabies for extinction.
        Believe me, I'm speaking
trying to monitor this breathing—it must be
        breathing—inhaling the part
of me that wants to look away. What then,
        and who, has turned my face to
rain?.

Refinery

Let the words fall, please just let them.
With all we've abandoned by now
chances are we could piece the fallen
city together by recall, assemble

the family members for a new portrait.
We could put the terror in reverse: how
the black chalk erases off the faces and the blood
returns from the salt water, filling

the scattered limbs that are assembling now,
back onto the bodies. How the boys, enamored,
amnesiac, stare down at their boots until

they board the ships and sail back the way
they came from, the sands left unstained,
apologies forgotten in their throats.

Lines Where the Fence is Crossed

Begin with *Are you for me*
or against me, for me
or against
    a backdrop, that's all.
Any hero ragged,
    Any border owned
And only your dog or your tears to hold you up
—"right."

* * * *

Bury my heart in me,
all's I ask.
There's an electric wire
round the family portrait,
the smiles our faces bore
to give our fathers reason.
The old Ford, metal he earned
his face blank for, long ago
compressed to bright
scrap in the yard.
Ashes, son, ashes, daughter.
1924 was a mill yard
and I was its dust,
the arc from there
to the tree you sit under,
my unparalleled splendor,
my preflight in a dusk too choked
to see through, my dalliance,
sweethearts, through the last innocent war.
I did what I was told
and I did it my own way.

* * * *

Luck was a lady
but I knew better.
We were luck,
crammed in the backseat,
landscape our eternity
shifting through the window.
Everyone was as good as us,
but no one knew the lines.
Your love hangs a worm
from a bluebird's beak,
tell me who isn't hungry?
How did you go on giving
all from your own dry mouth,
your sorrowing breadcrumb,
my love, yes, my assault,
sprung near the end of the day.

* * * *

If you say a man
is absurd to run
reciting his horror
magnificently each morning
into the judicial mirror,
what will you say to rain?
Will you lift the piano
to prove you didn't fear?
I'm not saying I might not help
you on a given day, but usually
I don't muster that particular
kind of stamina.
His noise is my life's sentence.

* * * *

Here. Stalin's son couldn't stand his luck,
his father's or his own, no matter.
Maybe the electric fence
was buzzing a lullaby
ooh ah ooh ah ooh ah
a croon so deep in his chest
all he had to do was

* * * *

Your father's driving in a circle
with his head on his chest
and mother doesn't seem to notice.
You're telling her over and over
Again to *look* but it's your dream,
not mine. I'm trying to speak to you,
not to myself. I'm waiting by a break
in the fence for someone
to walk the pond with,
but tonight I'm unusually worried.
I want the evening to let up.
I want to keep talking
and urge the huge trout,
so algae-ridden they must
have been eating this pond
for years, to keep flipping
their dull silver into the air.
Every clumsy thud serves, somehow,
an edict against the thriving yellow
grass the wind blows through
with no sound. It doesn't matter
that no place remains familiar.
If I keep talking,
even here could be home.
There are lives I walk into
through a slight change in tone.
I don't think you'd call me a liar.
With nothing but desire to own,
a farmer with knee-high boots

and a three-legged dog limping down
the gravel road takes on a semblance
of me, or you. You might think
he'll shoot me, but I'm a woman,
a girl to him probably, mostly grown
anyway and nervously at ease.
Of course I can't say but
I think it'd all be the same
if I was a man or a boy.
Belonging implies possession
and the days I don't notice
even the echoing din of a garbage truck,
I think you could say I don't exist.

* * * *

My mother's art is not my own.
No snow ever fell that shade of blue
and the yellow light in the cabin window
is a comfort no one's ever owned, have they?
and even if they built it together, and for us,
inside, there were only four walls
to bump into so I ventured out,
stumbling.

* * * *

And came down from the crags
at a different time of day, then,
in another family, with much less talk
and nearly blind in the dark. And still
it was the same *10 minutes, 10 minutes,*
and we'll be there. . . . But where were we
until then . . . evergreen flanking
both sides, armed in this century's colorful
slash, meant to mark the trail home?

(for Sarah)

from *The Secularist* 1997

The Secularist

I know the staggering
    lights from the Hancock Tower
searing the river's face
    were the end of the story.

But in that light, stripped of candescence,
    sinking into the river's crawl,
I almost believed
    again, candle's flicker

spreading, in the underwater church,
    across the feet of the stewards,
across the money box
    where they dropped their love, across

the stone robes, and what we call *answers*,
    kept hidden there. In after
-thought: the light brushed finally
    the feet of the kind, dearly dead god.

I stood there often,
    fingering absence at the Charles'
edge. I considered
    my choices. There in that place

—what was it you called it?—
    "the spirit of matter"
raised its divining finger
    toward me. What do you do

with light you can't be quit
    of, throwing its gleam
on you from a holy grave
    you thought you'd dreamed

clear out of your sleep
    years ago? I'm trying to say
I didn't want that touch
    there in that imagined place,

couldn't want that touch
    here on the nearly ruined shore.
Behind me, in the real city,
    the coal muffles the birth
-cry of the woman

    cutting her own umbilici
in a single room. She wraps
    the slippery string around
the child's neck, kisses

    him once on the forehead,
and tightens. Do you hear
    her prayers mumbled rapid
-fire? The spirit of matter

    scratches its ass against
a brick wall. I know
    if I stay here
let the light drift

    slowly across me
I could feel love.
    But, I'm going to go home.
I'm waking up in my own bed.

Something to Keep

Because this began from love,
a whisper in passing, approval
lighting her hair. Here is where
my name steps in, *Claudia*,
from the Latin meaning
lame, calling come home come home
I will hold us safely together,
we will consider the falling whole.
Cripple with an empire of days
attached to her body.
Do you know enough to say it
the parts ask, do you love
enough to reveal us, paper,
flesh, the face of the rain
on the microscope's slide,
your one good eye?
Nothing ever again free
from the collusion of my entry,
climbing the bus stair promising
to let it all wash over me,
swearing to let it all wash over me
so I may give it back, intact.
All the eddying qualities snarling
in the narrow aisle air,
if I can just be quiet,
not resist them,
let them wash over, not into, me
won't this be ours then?
Won't there be room then,
for my omissions,
his intention to kill,
her three bags of personal sorrow,
the driver's final, unspoken fear of his job?
I need to ask you now, teacher,
why it's destination you defy.

See, I'm on the bus regardless,
some kind of collage of coal and grief,
and sometimes a bird, or the wind,
threading *here* to that other *there*
makes me especially anxious to arrive.
Does the God we believe in want us,
howling and dirty from the listening?
How will I ask forgiveness now,
driving this packed bus
to the only *where* I know?

Armistice

The preflight of the sweet jets.
The public dying down below.
I was left
a private woman, a discreet investigation.
How did I come to assume
the other's day? His walking against traffic, her upturned hand,
all the voices spilling hair
into my mouth while I slept? There's a rock the harbor fears.
It bleats in the crooked arm of time
spent until you see them now, but turn away forgetting.
Starvation carving its form
into even the most unwilling.

* * *

In hell, it is they who first come
forward to meet Ulysses, their transparent bodies
a story without comment: "Women workers: Mimi,
Tolstoy fan, my coworker
in iron bars, Mimi's sister,
mother of the burned kid."
And later, lyrical heartbreak, arc
of history: "Male workers: violinist,
conceited blonde,
singer at the furnace,
boy with mallet,
my fiancé,
his brother."
Elsewhere, here in the sound of the flypress, on the street
and opposing traffic, she places her malformed hands.
Their utility.
"Pity and mute indignation of neighbors."
Brothers, Sisters. Blank God.
A laying of but you will not touch me.

* * *

Elsewhere, here
in the sound of the flypress, on the street and opposing:
"We must make a new public investment."
Elsewhere,
the possibilities of fire and ice.
Feb. 16, 1991: Anthony C. Arguello, 51,
of blank, shot his estranged
wife at blank,
then used the gun on himself.
Under the moon's face, here
in the sound of the flypress,
on herself blank god turns
under the gun himself,
the possibilities of the moon's face
O fire O ice O
pity and mute.

* * *

Not blank, not sleeping,
but helpless: the harbor
feeding its form,
the rock-sunken god
mute and water, and the millions
turning a profile
toward your city. She's armless,
Venus of this,
faltering under their stare.
I could leave,
abandoning your body:
April 8, 1991: Martin Drew, 27,
shot and killed his estranged
But my feet in this mud
Nov. 11: Laytona Lynnet Logan
shot and turning the O gun
   My body.

* * *

That year they were flagless
and she thought yes,
this is it, right here
that course, butterflies
pinned to white, a jet through an adulterer's
hour, skaters punctuating the flaming
   ROSE on the laborer's chest
and what after all still left.
   In the heartbreak of her year:
"The important thing is to be nothing."
Though what she had come to resemble then
was something entire.

* * *

That which disappears
and saith unto him: teacher
and saith unto her: touch me not,
sympathy and her object
not deferred but subject
to *partage*, light
and the integrity of a prism.

Demography

Because angels are in a holding pattern somewhere, I'm sure,
    but this is a different country. All the music you hear
on a certain station is good, its promise filling and filling the
    car, despite the road's absence of a shoulder, a frontage road
You could hear better by. Yes, it's good though
    something here would force those notes into the red end the trees
proffer. It's only the body history remembers, the horse
    that killed Catherine the Great, the star, dimly on the
Christmas tree and everybody at your door: *Is that a real
    star, what's that smell, I don't see my name here, etc.* One day
the oxygen disappears in the tree's length and you throw it out
    in June, shreds of tinsel trailing across the sidewalk.
If I could pray I'd ask to want less here,
    to take the stray arm flung into the air of a city
street as proof enough. Once, walking into a café
    where I worked, the day's possibility so spread through me
I could almost finger its golden wires, Isaiah, another
    exile in a kitchen of America, threw down his broom and
breathed—I can only say *from*—my neck so deeply, we both
    nearly fainted. But we didn't. We held our ground.
Instead, the music I heard again today between us,
    we danced, each taking turns with the broom.
Oh, how we enter the story and that character is its flaw.
    It suffices to say, we were both so far from home, our dance was it.

The End Is an Animal

The hole the day digs for your feeling is opening now.
    Let it go. Let it go or follow it in, kicking
over the precipice—what does it matter?
    It's not yours anymore.
Puddles deepen in this sudden thaw, a hand lifting
    —do you feel it?—from your mouth, breath stabilizing,
you call this the spirit of the matter? Nothing huge
    and old and incredibly wise is living
under the field somewhere. And what drifts against
    your throat sometimes—oh, pity it. Muttering, weak God,
patron of aneurysm, production lines, patron
    of food banks and cool water, dear intelligence!
Dear Gnosis, most holy note: For weeks now, driving in my car,
    attempts to know the story pouring from the announcer's mouth,
I've felt your bruised will sobbing from the periphery of the road.
    I swear it was your soundless agony hurling from the tree line,
to the houses' small lights, and back. You passed through the car
    and I couldn't touch you. Teacher, the body of God is a mass grave.
In him the souls are reeling and he is rocking them now in the grass
    and calling us by name. Under the shifting clouds,
he is rocking and calling our names. In the hole,
    birds thread straw through the eyes of your feeling.
She is the loneliest of girls, having forgiven your abandonment.
    She is the body keeping you from yourself, from God.

She cringes at your interrogations, she is a flesh lampshade,

    she is a million ID tags, she is the sensation inside your bones.

She is all that is true, beautiful girl, taken into a coma by one

    after the other, into death and still they won't leave her.

And when you mumble *Why God?* it is her face, not his, that kisses

    your lids to sleep. Hear her whisper *It's not his fault.*

Ave Verum Corpus

It occurred in the spaces the community choir left in the new
    concert hall. The body the composer was trying to make, I mean.
In those four minutes, hovering, but finally only *there* as they left,
    American and amateur in the black clothes required.
My people leaving on crutches, in columns, single file,
    until their absence, the thing he must have wanted,
stark against the sandalwood wall. By comparison,
    the next, busy violin, gratuitous applause.
We'd been finally West, our figures in the old building's light
    projecting from the cliff onto the ocean, unappeased. So far from
our bodies there, weren't we so far, I believed we might gladly
    touch there, until I recalled how touch looked in the painting,
the century's comment on intimacy, our spotlight's hypodermic,
a clarifying virus. Gone, though we looked all through the museum
    for it. I'd known where it was but even its wall was gone
and I was afraid for the theft. Between vision and love, too much beauty.
    A woman miscarrying in a high hotel room and each time
she opens her eyes again, the people in the building across the street,
    opening windows, smiling out into the brick face, each time
a new body and its morning. And then the possibilities
    of the traffic jam, the bridge a harp thick with not speaking.
The American choir singing our body.

3. Word (from "Beloved")

Want to say, you know, can we
get along? Can we get
Um, can we stop making it,
making hard   It's just not
it's not right I love—
I love every—
I'm not like they're
got to quit you know after all I mean
It's just not right   those people
never home again I mean we're all
stuck here for   let's you know
I love   I'm every   I'm not like
um want to say not right
not like they're not me
um know I mean stuck here
let's you know work   mean   out
stop hard making
to quit after
all I mean
never home again not like please
hard stuck I mean

Parable 2

Because when she dreamed the Madonna always rode the donkey
and he and the governess walked ahead leading the way
through the mountains. Beautiful, the mountains, even
real, Indian Paintbrush the red word caught, even
Franco in his coffin
pulling a certain loyalty
here in her image civilization,
the gas disguising the shower,
the child renaming the bomb,
India disguising the woman washing her hair
in a dark stream. Oh, what she wouldn't give
was her best resistance, Bastille,
fallen snow, Berlin, hell even the Alamo
bleeds in this. Between war and marriage,
seduction offered from ugly American cars,
tuberculosis this year's cure,
the neon truth of the woman
voulez-

  vous

   danser

AVEC

moi

   ?

the photographer's face gazing back at herself
from a mirror on the floor.
I did not choose to be blind, to see
only how they'd managed in their way

to turn her into a statue, to spray-paint

and piss on, late, much later, than then.

I wept for the governess,

her rope-burned hands, her casualty of skirt.

I loved him then but didn't know the words he sang

until I spoke them today, in the clear high bone of your cheek.

Parable 5

On the outside, like you,
of the public garden, the well-kept secret
not held in my hand.

                              I saw today a face
in the duck pond that was never mine.
I wanted to love the face
but the water was a body
strewn with feathers.

Kindness is overfeeding the ducks today.
It is arranging
the flowers into a wall.

Promenading its muscle,
the world clenches—your feeling.

I'm trying to resist the way it works,
wire holding up the water's rock,
a border mending the flowers into a wall,
the circle I walk here
without a name.
I'm leaning against a tree,
its life taking place underground.

* * *

And then there was nothing
    and shadow straddled

the imaginary dirt unmaking
    love in the zero hour.

There was a password
    traced in the invisible

passage the summer birds
    erased as they flew.

No feather fell into her open hand,
    there, in the primary light

of blankness,
    in the absent stutter the neon wrote

in the street-less anathema where
    she failed to cry: *Un-name me.*

And Its Discontents

The spirit is moving

the surface of the water

today, a school

of fish by light,

all mouth and forward

thrust, all mouth. What I can't see—

the body of a fish—and so

am drawn to light, blurring

the distinctions between in

-side and out, the mile

of surface light they wake,

lost now behind the trees.

Something mercenary promised.

The mouth of the withheld

open with laughter.

Saint Anthony witnessing to the caught,

strung things, emptied of motion

there on the dock. Old voices,

old stories. Shoal,

shoal, mouthing near the edge of a shallow.

But that was years ago.

What is retrieved, illusion,

God's finger a larger

form of water, manifest

most likely, in the tracings

the heart monitor or lie

detector would like to reveal. What is inside

spreading itself all over things,

the fishes' light-plagued, staccato

jumps, the beginning

of a machine's war,

or a version of rainbow.

      Outside, debris,

week's end. The fish

too silver and other to be real

from the beginning. But the bird, this morning,

stunned by the window's half-truth,

flight passing from sight.

It stood and stared, not like bird,

but something shapeless, older and more

patient, for an hour until shadow

forced it back to name

then to motion then to—Neither instinct nor action!

A bird crooned is illusion,

is elsewhere, an effigy of time.

I live alone, have no neighbors

though my love gathers crumbs

in the next room

and the old caretaker bleeds

our well, burns the old grass.

My body knows us,

withering into its truth, a statue

in a public garden.

In time, the catastrophes weren't enough.

The believers burn again

in the family hour, the hurricane

a form of fan,

the body a word collapsed

under a flag.

Writing was in its origin

the voice of an absent person.

In one hand, a basket of fish,

in the other a ticket, or letter.

A little closer somehow.

from *Utopic* 2000

Toccata with Child

I came in from under the music
a Thursday
far to go *etc.* pulling out all the stops
until Sunday when it started again
in five voices
and I saw I was a woman
feeding her son
on the inside, somehow,
(a Thursday)
everything but nothing
pushing against the shape I made
(a woman) bent toward an open mouth
specific hunger calling the day
I wanted to wake in
listening to cacophony
and then I heard no longer
(until Sunday) when it started again
in a single voice
and I saw everything but nothing
in the (specific hunger) small body
asking me to *wake up* and listen
from Thursday and each
day (until Sunday) and starting begins again
I hear it, small specific body,
inside (a door slams) somehow hungry in the music
playing in all the stops

Bluff City

"The same indignation that is said to have cleared the temple once will clear it again . . . It seems as if no one had ever died in America before; in order to die you must first have lived . . ."
—Henry David Thoreau
A Plea for Captain John Brown

But it still doesn't explain why

                it took the passive

resistance form too.

                I was eight when he died in this city.

Dying on the outside, the gunshot

                of that year killing the inside

of what constitutes my/our

                "The method is passive physically

but strongly active spiritually."

                In that I had a way of seeing

attached to my feeling

                paralyzed at the beginning

of Being.

                "It is not the suffering

but that which comes from outside

                which is remedy."

(the method)   (the paralyzed will)

(of a child)   (of a nation)

"We talked about it in India

                and in Africa but the American

movement was—

unpremeditated, a natural,

                a religious."

(meant staying inside)   (a child)

(inside)   (a nation)

In that I had a way of seeing

attached to my feeling

where the world wouldn't start

immobilized

(inside a child nation)

"Then Moses said, 'The kids are

dead.'"
"It is not the suffering

but that which comes form outside

which is remedy."

The kids are dead.
(a child)
(of a nation)

"And the other thing is

people were being killed

already, the Negroes

of Mississippi and I feel,

anyway, responsible."

"For while the nonviolent resister

is passive,

his mind and emotions

are always active."

At the beginning

of Being.

[W]riters themselves always try to lessen the distance between their kind and ordinary human beings, they so often assure us that every man is at heart a poet, and that the last poet will not die until the last human being does."

                              In that I had a way of seeing
attached to my feeling
                              and when I couldn't see to feel,
I ceded the day to event.
                              Or I lost the trajectory
of the hours
                              huddled in a stingy minute
thought in a sound loop
                              the music all wrong
though I'd given it away, my feeling
                              willingly, by the handful.
History is the gap
                              through which the lessons fall:
"Moses said, 'The kids are dead.'"

In that I had a way of seeing
attached to my feeling
but the dead bird, just there and there
until I picked it up with a shovel
and buried it in the street.
            Its end written already, a thousand worms, a coat,
or jeweled shroud so that the leaves I pushed
over what remained of its body
seemed unholy or I did,
performing last rites without the benefit of a bell or veil,
empty of blessed words. A false priest with a shovel
an evening falling/an evolution of the bodiless

/the decayed interior of a bird
the medium where I began to understand:

when he hit her
       bringing the heel of his hand down
across the bridge of her nose
       it's safe to say he felt her skin
as an extension of his own
       the slight pop the bones made shattering
hardly in competition with the sirens, the flight patterns
       much less the—roaring? or simply the language?—
of his psyche, because he was all inside, he must have been,
       ignoring the streetlight, the dogs and other people
walking and then shouting, his hand, that instrument rising
       almost detachedly, higher and higher
until the force was clean and attached to intention.
       There is no safety in saying.
The wallet then almost a distraction
       and the way he ran away
"trying to lessen the distance between"
       (loping, looking over his shoulder)
"their kind"
       (soul depicted)
"and ordinary human beings"
       at the heap she made in the street.
Two boys skate over the spot today.
       A black man they say
and they're ready for him
       holding tree branches in their hands.
It's warm and green shows in the brown.
       When I look again

they've tied the sticks together
        and are sailing into town.
Bluff City.
Even without the windows open
        I've been dreaming
behind bars that face the neighbor
        my sleep has made
whole again.
        I've resisted his story,
hurried inside to stop him
        depicting the apparatus
of event and time
        that left his body crushed
from the shoulders down.
        He believes
that touch, in Japanese,   R

              E

              I

              K

              I
can keep you in this world
        and a nurse has slipped into mine,
simply the word "nurse"
        and the hands she lay
on his forehead
        15 years ago.
(who believes in touch cannot)
        (who cannot believe must)
I am reading the underlined
parts of *Heal Your Body*
by Louise L. Hay he slipped

onto my porch:

SPINAL MISALIGNMENTS

5-C Fear of ridicule and humiliation   *I lovingly release others to their*
                                                own lessons.

Fear of expression.
Rejecting one's good.   *I lovingly care for myself.*
Overburdened.   *I am loved.*
                                                And I am safe.

In the dream I might have had
he has reclaimed his name, Butch,
and he and the two boys
drive three to a cab,
two sticks, a gun and the intentionality
of a city,
fuchsia scripture
mending earth to sky.
(God bless what is broken, what cannot move,
God bless the reflection that is harmless
unattached to desire,
the minor delusions
that strengthen our humanity)

Lessen the distance

In that the outside disappeared completely
into the limbs of his body
so that when I see him in his chair in the sun
I know that it's day.

No dream possible
                      he's back (we're
back), or a version of us
                      "looking into your window with a knife" or further
down the street
                      "back from the army and looking for a friend."
Something subdued,
             halted in the weight lifter's
             STOP THERE OR I'LL SHOOT
(I'm not kidding)
                  In the neighborhood's WATCH GROUP,
the names, the numbers we exchange.

Night in the flight patterns the steamboat
crying the violence turned
outward and upstairs, his cry/her cry
mine/the small boy's/night of the wheelchair
and the eyes he turns
to the stars at the end of the drive.
Night of nothing seen or felt,
the cries protracted in the spine
and the silence, the aftermath
protracted and protracted,
the whole body fed by it,
severed by the sleeping child.

The religion in expression,
             true or false. Religious tanks
moving up Poplar Avenue,
             religion of curfew,
the monuments to memory
             something wants to wreck.
The moot dismemberment
             of Christ *again*,
in her arms, in Rome
             so you see now there is nothing
left to recall but the shape
             they write in the body.
Genetics suffering history,
             cattle car lowing toward
the museum. All the responsible pictures
             promising your children
sitting, or standing, a place on the train.
             I would like to invite you to lunch
I am your age
             The world is a place I would like to step off of
There is forgetting to do
             in my church
Been disabled,
             enjoy I think, common interests?

"You asked what happened to Rosa.
I think I can tell you.
You know the law
you say, well,
let's fight it.

It's that. That's
just the whole attitude.
A time when you decide you don't give a rap.
I don't live in_____
but I'm in_____
and I know why people fell in."

(a child)   (of a nation)

She walked alone.
                    (at the corner)(I tried to pass)
(through)   (the guards the crowd)   (was quiet)
                    (I tried to squeeze)   (past him)
(he raised his)   (bayonet)   (and they raised their)
                    (bayonets)   (somebody yelling lynch
and lynch her)   (Drag her to the etc.)
                    (the branch seemed safe to me) (a white lady)
(very nice)   (put me on the bus)   (a white man)
(patted me)   (raised me)   (said don't let them
                    see you cry.)

But it still doesn't explain why
it took the passive
-resistance form it took

(I tried to squeeze) (past)

We talked about it in India
and in Africa but the American movement was—
        unpremeditated, a natural, a religious. Over.

(And he raised his) (And they raised their)

I had not begun not believing

in a center, a self's

or this city's but thinking

to make one or find

one or only to find

one in the making.

What I love

I left singing

in the student gallery,

the elevator rising

away from the music I continued

to hear until I stepped off

in another place.

You divisible in the notes

you whistled among the bad

sculptures and I—

feet traveling a hallway. Song forgotten

and the elevator's ascent away

from what you had become—only a point,

not fixed but a *point*—not ever

a place to return to.

This city's quick descent

to the Mississippi not a simile

for anything related to us,

as the bridge cannot

be a freedom stretching west

from the city of two dead kings

where last night the sun

fell into the river and shared

its light a while before

it went away.

The method is passive physically but strongly active spiritually.
(I tried to pass)   (was quiet)
The aftermath creation of the beloved
(and he raised his(and they raised their
And aftermath creation of endless bitterness
(patted me(raised me(said(don't let them
see you
I hadn't known it would be a motel
on the edge of Memphis, turning away until he said, No, there.

The Lorraine Motel, Rm. 306,

a wreath over the number
we were forced by the architecture
to start on the outside,
to start at the end
of Martin's life, the well-photographed
balcony leading

                 se

                    quence of

                 a a meta

                      morphosis of the

                 vis oral   cul

                      ture and religious

                 tradition

                 to insure the retaining of an

                 a leg   acy

in nerve, in language on to Rosa's bus
and the inside of his room,
artificial coffee memorialized in black plastic
If there is no struggle there is no
progress   Am I not a sister

Memphis, 1996

Gravity & Grace

1.

À fin   all was strange   of my heart
     a landscape   of I am not
Disappearing, things   became perfect

Once   to hear, see, touch   eat
     deprived God   something saying
A landscape   disappearing   in I am not

Now perfect   disappearance   appearing perfect
     see hear   *sear*   touch not
a landscape *fin*   in I   of I am not

2.

If my window   is red   I cannot see

      anything   but rose   accord

to rose   the window   to revolt

Mountains, rocks   fall upon us   Hide us

      far   I deserve this   wrath

the red principle   of revolt   the rose

Room the red window   Violence

      trains view   Mountains, rocks   fall

train wrath   Tho' I die   doing

3.

Suffer	suffering	to reduce it
Not sacred enough	Being and others	
Rock upon	the obstacle	the rock

Suffering spread	beyond reduct	-ion
Sacred good	or beautiful thing	an insult, then
Being inside rock	transformed mud	& others

Forgive	the void beautiful	in being
a branch	to a drowning	future
Sacred enough	or not	Writing

forgiveness

4.

Good broken up into   pieces
          a host of women   /or of men
I leaves marks   on the world it destroys

Broken good   never anything new   everything
          equivalent   a host of   /or of
I was your friend   once

Lost Her   knowing good but hating good
          She broke into   equivalent pieces
I held Her   lost good

In a broken   factory   a single tear
          destroyed Host and Host
                                  I destroyed

Preserving Her

Blue Diamond

I am virtually gone

                              author or victim

I wanted   in you   to be nothing

          to be a solitude

attached   by emptiness   to everything

Last night   one coyote

                    this morning two

They were nature

Keep the children close

                    author or victim

The desert looks flat, lies

       flat   what does realism save?

They were animals running across the surface

They are gone

Oar

I had wanted to describe the river but
        away   in the distance   on two sides
                see the banks

The river fills the propellers   Neither the river
       nor the ship is mine & in the distance
                see the banks

The virtue I wants is none

Confession is a broom
the surface cleaner than before

I wears my fellows beings,
the surface stranger for confession

The pages amply prove repression
              is violence
the pages in prohibited areas
             violence

I's disobedience is a preparation
      for more suffering
        unperceived   gentle
homage to ourselves

Embers

Apologize for birth &
       convey more being
What is true outside
is equally true inside
Apologize and convey
Believe unprovoked suffering
       speaks unrivaled
silent suffering
       speaks unrivaled
It is solid work   it is always true

Debts: Before the Afterword

"Je est un autre" is still the largest proposal ever made, long before and after Rimbaud's beautiful sentence, by Jesus, Simone Weil, Martin Luther King, Jr. and many others. It is too simple; it is too complex, its concept of unity suffused with the agony of disunity, suffused with the single imperative of meeting oneself *in* oneself and *in* the other. Just as saintliness is unnatural in the willing mortification of the flesh, and passive resistance is unnatural in its acceptance of pain and death for the betterment of the whole, so there is in the violation of language's conventions, a wholly unnatural inclusiveness to be forged. Method as a means and end unto itself is an instrument of hallucination; Gandhi's urging people to accept the repeated blows of the British seems an act diabolical at worst, irresponsible at best, without the ideality of Indian equality he believed would result from the act. Similarly, experiments with breath, noun, pronoun, tense, case, punctuation, etc. must not be experiments interested only in the "materiality" of language but experiments dedicated to finding, at the level of the syllable, what *life* has been left out or erased in dominant culture's acceptance of conventional language modes. Such poetry is made of notes, without hierarchical but strictly relational value, a poetry whose ethos, like music's, is indiscriminate in the best sense. Inside of it, a center is ever emerging, a center which is, nonetheless, rooted in the song's initial movement; its sense accrues in what is added—and erased—from its original motif. Inside of it, the true is ultimately improvisational but is the original impulse. Just as King's aim in accepting imprisonment was to de-center, to de-stabilize status quo by calling existing hierarchies into question—; as Simone Weil's refusal of the designation "Jew" was the beginning of a secular and religious experiment that still disturbs orthodoxy; as Gandhi's lifelong commitment to destroy the designation "untouchable" written into his religion made him suspect in the Indian world; so the degree to which such poetry succeeds will depend upon an addition to—and erasure from—existing definitions of poetry. *Las Vegas 2000*

from *The Devotion Field* 2004

Critical Essay

Anyone writing can come to know
Everything one reading does

Anyone reading might never know
Everyone one writing does

If anyone is really writing
Anyone is really reading

Anyone knows everything writing
Everything anyone reading might never

Anyone for example I I found writing
The experience of the dead gods you

Read in Jane Harrison's *Prolegomena*
The gods dead and gone already in Greece

At the moment Orpheus is born
I for example I found writing the empty

Alpha where the beginning died and I
& Anyone for example Anyone finds writing

Truly writing the end's beginning the empty
Alpha full of the gone God's writing

The Scarlet Letter

> "I don't like it when I find myself responding to what
> somebody else has written. . . I'd rather respond to
> something I know nobody wrote, like a puddle . . ."
>
> —THYLIAS MOSS

After I left the scaffold I walked
through the crowd, rights gone,
the texts they quoted yelling after me
meaningless beside my own blood Alpha,
and her fleshy perfection screaming swaddled

                              in my arms.

I saw my future, my Angelhood, sprung
from the imagined book of my author—

Not the Great American Novel you held sweating,
angry inside your incomprehensibility
in high-school classrooms—

But that tale of choice and retribution
only history, not poetry, could record.

Poetry bounced against the impenetrable wilderness
attempting nature, but She was artifice.

She caressed the gaps of my story,
my author's inability to love or to hate me.

I, on the contrary, was free inside
my demarcations and systems,
breath by line by heart by step
leaving the settlement—
You see how it is with me.

Even the hair I tucked
into my cap was a concept,
each sun, struck strand hidden
one of the . . . the ambiguities
your world continues to hover erotically around,
fingering the silkiness.

"The angle and apostle of the coming revelation
must be a woman . . . " yes,
& I'm achieving Art, disembodied
inside the footsteps

that stepped then into a puddle—
ugh, who wrote *that*?

Shallow, natural hole,
a surface with a mirror,
all the townspeople's looking

crowing out my form
as they gazed in steerage
from that earthly hole.

Via Negativa

You had nothing, you said,
Though all of our life
You'd reminded me that there is no
Such thing as nothing
In nature, so naturally
The grasshoppers drowned in the pool.
It was my job to net them
Until nothing remained
But the shadow of wings on water.

I opened some books and stole some words.
Here, put them back.
I opened a door and stole some air
So—breathe.
No, you don't know what I mean.
I've only seen one movie,
The one where the boy wags
The plane's wing
Over his mother's house
To say he is well,
And encouraged by shadow,
She gives meat and milk
To a young German boy
Who will not thank her.

You think you can get off the movie set?
You'd better count your lucky something's.
Some people's lives are, moment to moment,
A live shot of a car explosion
In one of the countries where they hate you,
And the rest of the world, believe me,
Is marching with signs of their approval.

Not everyone loves Jesus or Uncle Tom,
But I do, sweet suffering Christ,
I love them and I love you too,
Generally and specifically,
So march on over here
And let's have some love,

(Put your sign down, I say,

Lay down your v__nity)
You sorrowful monkey, you.

A movie set or an ocean . . .
Sorry to get metaphysical on you . . .
I'm physical about the metaphysical:
Coming from and/or in an ocean . . .
You come too!
And if you insist on staying there,
All alone in your blanket,
Jesus or Uncle Tom or I
(You come too!)

Will rock you in our arms
And the ocean will be your bed
O sorrowful and suffering . . .
The cries of the monkeys on the movie set
So distant now,
We leave our shadows and follow

Poetry Anthology

Don't worry about the lost children
They're not lost
No more than you reading this in your underwear
Is it time to go already?
I heard it in the voice of the cartoons
It starts with that kind of exaggeration
& gets louder if you don't shut it off
Don't look for God in the details
S/he ululates in the beetle's wing
You plastered their faces on papers any killer could see
& Criminalized their father
Stealing & stealing & stealing y/our love

You complained bitterly about it
Wanted to know exactly the smell and taste
   Ascribed but you were the problem

Not it

You put it in a frame
You called it the age
There were motorcyclists there
& Sawed-off shotguns
The motorcyclist fell down
The shotgun killed the teacher.
See what you did?
All the lost children crying under a flag
My country 'tis of thee

My Liberace

In your spangled lees I sing

Perpetua   Perpetua   In Perpetua

oh   mo   doh moh   doh moh

Art in heaven

WEANED from your name

Gather me   the surface turned rote

Gabardine ruined all my care

Because he's been to the desert

On a horse with No

Maine, Henry David and the Indian

Racing with canoes on their heads

Couldn't find Margaret Fuller   She drowned

& her baby too went down

My region's asunder

In and out of book and ache and place

Beetled and a black dog

Daddy take your paw

Seeking easy millennium

Oh the mass

Oh the mass

Oh the masticating maw

T'is of Thee

The pictures took over
& Time was film
No music   Only Flags
I heard their waving
By the plum's furry blight
O early dawn
Midday *Après midi*
All day   Every day
Our lady of the shopping cart
Peering through the wire link
Search the depths for a map:
My country for a map!
Where the proper road 'tis a horse
And a dog who sniffs
Out the killer hiding under a bush
Pinning a note upon him which saith:
"The truck stops here"
Midday *Après midi*
All day   Every day
A film around the sun
& "Earth's Summit" not a found vista
But a meeting
Where the third world
Holds dead stars in their hands
& the Secretary of State
Is "doing our very best"

To get a hold of his emissions
I'm leaking with laughter
Our lady of the shopping cart has a nosebleed
In the film, death entered
The guest room and stayed
Not a character but a sound
This roaring in the ears
Which was anthem
As motif gains power
When in the tide
She's released from the ship
State that held her.

Hello Beloved

"[W]hen my life is over
It'll be just as over as hers."
—ALICE NOTLEY

I thought my body
Was for other uses
A prayer instrument   A music vehicle

Nothing as simple as a tunnel

I played with here there

Traditional, singular,
Tradition of lone-livingness
A singularity vocation vacation
          Trace of

Emily Brontë, Hester Prynne,
others—Not mystic,
Alone and with child (inside the world)

What is kindness for?

Veronica washing his feet

Mary's arms

The erotics of absence

I brought to our love affair

Erotics of *raison d'être*

My pearl you estranged me

Once, in the tunnel

Close in the mud

Both of it and *it*
There were pilgrims there misnaming
Something caved in
A lot of scrambling to the surface
Your face

I wonder if you can tell me, Eva Perón,
Why when the crumbling stopped
It was the waiting
Yes, in the terminal we used
To dig out?

Once thrown a rope
Mistaken for a basket
No One was happy
In her homemade house of reeds

No One misses the point

But the stars above her head
Pointed everywhere
& Looking she saw crushing
Grief past, demarcations
Strewn and uh-oh

I missed a lot
Never except in seconds
Loved specifically
Accepted an exit role
And called it nature

I'm not grateful for
What bullshit—The Grateful Dead
(Neither are they)
That's what my childhood rolled into
Gave up dope
But won't turn in my hacky sack

Kicking inside the Godhead
Kicking inside the work
Instead of—I don't know—
Existence—But then
I was placed outside at birth
So were you—Erotics of definition—
Existence and ecstasy
Derived both from the same root,
e.g., Instruction: "to live"
Is to be outside
Of now, this body,
Whatever noun you want
To place on it.

I fell
In love.
Stood back up. Married you.

Southern Anthology

& Sometime later I am on an airplane
Thinking about prison narratives,
How very attached one can become
To prison narratives,
Since, in all I've read, the release
Is assured from the beginning
Or at least by page thirty-six,
There is the eventuality of release
And the poignancy and good humor
Of the prisoners, incarcerated unjustly . . .
They are freer than we are, dear,
Staring at the pine trees
In the piney woods in Alabama,
Planning the future and the old age
We know will come with it.
I wanted to be a red lake
And I was for a while,
I was a red lake and people
Told stories, even myths sometimes
Over picnics by me.
And then *poof*, I was listening to the radio,
I was the radio, in 2003
& the announcer spoke politely
And it had come to pass
That in forty years segregation
Was virtually the same in the Northeast
And the West, though not in the South

Anymore, as in 1963 & Selma &

Birmingham and all the holy lands

Of the dark and piney woods clustered near red lakes . . .

Fog came into the prison then

Fog, as they say, a thick carpet of it,

Though nothing like that, just fog,

A cloud chamber, a spate

Of time under pressure of air &

Water and voices all speaking

In one, twanging, incomprehensible language—

O Sophia cried.

O Sophia spread her hair

Across the dark skyline

And cried.

"Though I am gone," she said

Through her gelatin tears, "though

I am irremediably gone (for now)"

She said through her glycerin tears,

"The world will continue its craggy story

And I will hope you hear it

From time to time."

The snow winked happily in the snow mound.

And "the mound" in Tuscaloosa

Sinks suddenly away from monument

Into the earth, Black Warrior

Shedding his name.

The prison door, too, has avoided monument.
I touched it but was not allowed to enter
& As surely as Martin left the urinal
And narrow bed, his speech in hand,
Left for his eventual assassination,
We left the museum
And walked out through the narrow door
Into the possibilities of the next page,
Or more nearly, another day.

You Are My Sunshine, My Only

You are my son-shine,
my lost Shoshone,

I skin a *beau fleuve*
in your heart

If there is tripartite,
I can't be sure, dear,

Another name for *deer*
is *hart*.

A judge lay weeping,
his robes were skewed, dear

His robes a Buff'lo
inside a park.

Inside the hair, dear,
the missing part, dear—

He turned to bread there
and there, he died.

Summer Anthology (Ives)

I was not after all interested
In the reality of the unseen.
The propaganda, the propagandists,
Of Spirit. Spirit is, uh-huh.
This is America, I see it.
America is not after all, interesting.
Places themselves aren't interesting.
Seeing is sometimes hearing.
Four boys on a Styrofoam raft
In a cove on Ozark,
D'eaux arc . . .
They ride its line
Fishing with bow & arrow
(Dock Squeak) (Wind Blows)
& later they anchor
The boat, tying a rope to the arrow.
America is not after all, interested.
These four boys are interesting
& The American music
Anyone hears if she's
Listening (Dock Squeak)
(Wind Blown)
Brown backs and white legs,
The Body Electric, a Styrofoam
Raft, arrow's the anchor
& All the other authors here
(Come back to the raft, etc.)
Your life now the (un) loaded

A. not after all interested
BANG! Deerslayer
An arc in their crazy
Paddling—the music you
Hear if you're listening
Well before the 4th of July
(Wind Blow) (Anchor Lift)
America is not interested after, etc.
Floating among the paper
Cups and beer cans,
Vesuvian dives BANG
These white-legged people
D'eaux arc can you see it
Fishing with (Dock Squeak)
No boat to speak of
They anchor, hidden in a cove.

Instead of Reading Marcus Aurelius

Not the night poem
Not that one
It was morning and the hummingbird moths
Were hunting in the bottlebrush
Not silence either nor absence
But the slow breathing of father and son
The books of others
Though not Hannah Arendt
The name she woke thinking
"I need to read Hannah Arendt."
All this before leaving
And more

Pill bottles with her name on them
Little bags of jewelry, of food,
A pen safe in a loop
The still air
And hummingbird moths flying through it
Hunting, he said, in the dawn
An enormous cup of coffee
And the slight unease inside her mouth
—Sharing their material?
Her intentions appreciated by strangers
The morning's rose gratitude

Lodged there, and rising, in her breath
Cerebral cortex there too
Which part of it loved music more than sight?

The hummingbird moths yes
But hardly their bodies (can't see them)
Rather the vibration of their—of what must be their wings?
The darting between the flame-red brushes
And what makes people laugh when they're not happy?
Registering that, feeling a crease on her brow,
Those sounds opposing each other
—Flying moth
—Laughing Lady traveler

The bronze face of the dead man in her lap
Who believed opinion was everything
And was ready to "accept without
Resentment whatever may befall."
Falling children.
Four out of five dead, except the "worthless Commodus
Who lived to succeed his father."
Hmm.
What would Hannah Arendt say
She wanted to know
The beauty of human enterprise, its folly, from above
Greening a desert
The indifference then and the glory
Of the red rocks
The human lines of a freeway
The wind trace on the small mountains
Nothing could live there
No, this a thought limited by a humanist idea of life
All the things she couldn't see living there below
Plants never yet classified
Scorpions and floating organisms

And O! A river!
The Colorado!
Not reaching its original destination
At last hearing, miles short of it
And its water "misting" the tourists at the casinos
O beautiful   O spacious
Your grainy grains of sand
Enjoying her belly for some reason
Enjoying the blue ink on the page
It's still there anyway, the Colorado
Long and skinny and in a canyon
Not the night poem
The day poem of travel
And people pointing
She's thoughtfully chewing her glasses' stems
Not thought   Not fully
Her teeth lightly on the plastic
How relevant! How marvelous and relevant!
She is in love with all the wonderful things
Teeth for example and biting
The floss sliding between the cracks
Smiles and snarls, as on a Ferris wheel
The English professor had said he didn't like those formless things
Speaking of Allen Ginsberg's poetry
And "Howl" the poem she was ready to teach again
All buttoned up with Jane Austen under his arm
And though it is true that candor abolishes paranoia
She did not say "Go to hell, fathead"
—Allen, dear man, wouldn't have wanted it—
But "good-bye" there on the stairs
Some things are desperate to be eaten

All the fine cereals in their boxes
The egg dishes she either chooses or does not
She's sleeping
The world below is full of rectangles
Farms are spreading across America
Trees come back and buildings
Nothing whispers in her ear
Sounds come in and out and in
She's awake for the second time today
Praise the open eye the awkward hands
The belly digesting the cereal
Praise the seat where she sits
Fly, Fly—Be a moth in your life
Be a quick movement among flowers
Bloom

from *Missing Her* 2009

Came Capsizing   the Human Boat

Came capsizing   the human boat

        Came lost   A warbird's face I wore

        Stolen by drowning

    We were an exodus

        Repeatedly in your airwaves

        Once I had a name

    Lost it   with my bird

    Capsizing beneath your heavens

Our own gods lost in the passage

        Your heaven was global

It was full of images

    The Earth was one of them

The Earth seen from space

    Still beautiful   Unreal as it was

In the pictures   Caribbean blue   Ionian white

    A ball you could hold in your hand

And they did   The companies who bought her

I died I guess free   Listening to a machine's whine

Somewhere above me

Pity Boat

I would not blow
        Into the tube
Of the life vest
Not in English
Nyet in Spanish
There were far too many ways to drown
Flying over Texas

        So I'm lying
Next to William Blake
In a big rubber raft
& he's teaching me how to love
Being dead. A slow study,
I fling my arms
After every cactus we pass.
"You're dumb, Claudia," Blake says.
"I am not," I say and poke
Poor William Blake
With a gun.
William Blake is beyond asking why.
And since the many and/or the few
Fuck everyone and/or thing they can
& since to fuck is to hit with a club,
He moved to Paradise.
I drive each day
Down Paradise Road
& one day I saw myself there.
I was 11 and I was crying

Running home through eucalyptus
To the El Granada motel.
Those trees knew the future,
Sweet tan bark
Shedding perpetually
In the salty air.
William Blake stretches out,
Happily naked and dead
In the what's next.
He's singing a song behind my eyelids
Somebody knows where we're going
William Blake is eating stars
& one, very slowly,
Brightens inside my mouth

Mary Wasn't Sure

Mary wasn't sure about any of it. She didn't like her traveling cloak
and she didn't like the donkey.

She didn't like the manger, or the shit that had lodged
itself on her shoe.

She didn't like the Kings and their smelly gifts.

She'd liked paying her taxes, and the sharp clatter the coins made
when counted, though she hadn't liked the journey, none of it, or all
the new villages one after the other withholding all the stories she'd
never hear or tell. She really didn't like the donkey that kept turning
its head and nipping her ankles. And she hated her traveling cloak.

She liked the angels and their sex-less-ness. Their vacant smiles
so full of promise. The sudden hope she felt when
they played their golden horns.

She wondered if she was an angel, but no, she had a baby. He lay in
a manger, no crib for his bed.

She liked the baby, its helplessness. His name was Jesus.
She wondered if he was an angel, but no, he was a baby. They, neither
of them, were angels. They were in it together, first of all
the manger, and then the rest of the story both she and Jesus already
knew. The shepherds, too. They knew and they liked the baby who lay
on her traveling cloak on the straw.

She didn't like the story, except the beginning, she didn't like the way
she knew how it was going to end, not because she already, as Jesus
already, knew the end, but because it was a tragedy, and she didn't like
tragedies. No one would remember this, the small and smelly
manger and the helpless baby who was clean and eating, who lay in
her traveling cloak on the straw. No one would remember her
as she was now, a girl who'd just paid her taxes and had a baby
she called Jesus, whom she'd bathed in a trough and lay
in her cloak on the straw.

She was a girl who'd just had a baby, she was happy, if a little tired,
and Jesus was happy, if asleep, but no one would paint this picture
enough. No, she saw it all, she knew it all already, and so did Jesus
in his baby sleep, dreaming himself the dead man his mother would
hold forever in her lap.

Little Elegy (American Justice)

The Banker's family

Was awarded

More than the Fireman's

& the Stockbroker's

More than the Cop's

The Insurance Man

Won out too, over

The small Rosa

Who dusted his many pens,

And all the way down

The many floors, the lives

Were rated, all of those

Who died September 11th.

What is Meant Here by the People

Problem with   "knowledge" including

    "Know-how"   including   "knowing how to live"

What is meant here by   "the people"

And who is one

What is meant here by the people and how to become one

I carried the heavy child across the river

I knew how   I meant to be a child

Including knowing how to live

And forgetting the lesser know how

What is meant here by the child

Excludes the possibility of the people

However well you know one

I know one

There is more

The river the currency   carried this child in me

Carried this knowing how to live

And was one

About Suffering They Were

I believed the linguist

On the radio who said words are most interesting

When they indicate something not there,

Something not inherently in or of themselves.

Freud thought of writing as the voice of an absent person.

I miss my father, and though I see signs,

I've begun to forget the sound of his voice.

So the roads come after, not before, which puzzled

The Japanese tourists on the architectural tour

In Harvard Square. Mercy, therefore, is made.

A Baedeker to follow, in any missing language.

A little embarrassing after all that no, there's nobody here

And her form too is continual instruction.

The new poem is the old master's painting.

Manifest suffering in every time zone

While father, as he must, goes elsewhere.

The old poem . . . There are no old poems,

Only new textbooks directing

The unprepared student to the painting

Behind the poem. I believe the phonemes,

Waking one day at last lost in the vowels

Of her dreaming.

Sleep me there.

The new poem is the sound

In the old master's painting.

We'll be tortured there,

Along with the animals

Whose suffering is mute

Or written in our missing language.

Father. Inconsequential me.

The feathers in our death.

Falling into yours.

Everybody's Autobiography

1.
At the end, the only thing left in my parent's house was the piano
and an oversize portrait of them on their wedding day.
At the end, he died in my house, in Las Vegas, and I called *I love you, Dad*

through moments struck open, a lid on a trunk that was our life together,
struck open, in his dying. At the end, the firemen and paramedics,
the coroner from Chicago smoking on the porch, and the captain saying

Would you like to pray? At the end, we did, struck open, the bed
that was his tomb still in the guest room, and yet no angel telling me
of the risen Lord. At the end, I kept returning to the room

to look at my father. In the end, they placed him in a bag, I heard
the zipping and though I didn't watch, I heard the effort they made lifting,
and he was gone, no sirens, before my son woke.

2.

In the beginning, in 1924, Lenin died, and Stalin ruled for 29 years.
Calvin Coolidge was president, and there was no vice president.
Clarence Darrow, a man who, unlike my father, believed in law, helped
Leopold and Loeb to escape the death penalty for the murder
of their 14-year-old cousin.

In the beginning, Ruth Malcomson from Pennsylvania was named
Miss America, and George Gershwin's Rhapsody in Blue
debuted in Paris.

On April 3rd, 1924, my father, Edward Thomas Keelan, Jr., was born
in Compton, California, to Marguerite Keelan, née Kearns, and Edward
Thomas Keelan, Sr., the boy between two girls, Peggy, 2, and Patricia,
the baby. This is the autobiography of everyone because all lives
and books begin and end.

              This is the autobiography of everyone
and is for all of us still alive in the broken middle-ness,
mouthing our stories.

              My father fell into this world from a woman's body.
              And yours?
  This is the autobiography of everyone
              because it was my father who taught me to distrust
              distinctions that separated the simple subject from
              the compound subject, particularly, and to begin with,
              the subject I. I'm hungry, I told my father.

    The world is rumbling, he said,
and placed a piece of bread in my mouth.

I'm thirsty, I repeated, and he pointed toward the split in the dream and handed me a hollow stick.

3.

Of death, Gertrude Stein writes in *The Geographical History of America:*

> Now the relation of human nature is this.
>
> Human nature does not know this.
>
> Human nature cannot know this . . .
>
> Human nature does not know that if everyone did not die
>
> There would be no room for those who live now.

This is true. Almost everything that Stein said was true.
I know because I've felt it happen, human nature.
Human nature is interested in itself.
One day, human nature finds a place—a room, a table, a field, a site
of becoming—where human nature loses, in a flash, first distinction,
and finds itself suddenly something other,
one's whole understanding of a glorious singularity
disappeared in an instant.

How large the world has become in your loss!
You have understood the purpose of death.
Having done so, you understand the purpose of life.
You must give your self away. Then you can sleep.
Stein: "This is the way human nature can sleep, it can sleep by not
knowing this. The human mind can sleep by knowing this."
I have spent my life asleep,

standing by the window year after year with my mother,
waiting for my father to come home safely.
This is the autobiography of everyone
asleep in one room or the other.
Natural mind, have you seen my father?

4.

In the beginning, Walt Disney created his first cartoon and another
invention, the Teapot Dome Scandal, debuted in Wyoming and Elk Hills,
California, not far from where my father worked the oil wells years later.

Harry F. Sinclair of Sinclair Oil Company was sentenced to prison
for contempt of the Senate and for hiring detectives to shadow members of
the jury in his case.

I like the dinosaur in the Sinclair Oil sign, just as I found
the oil wells themselves, perpetually making love
to the edges of Interstate 5, oddly comforting,
though a little sad.

In the years before my father was born, the Southern Pacific Railroad
monopolized California. William Hood was the chief assistant
engineer who saw that tunnels were the only clear route through
the sometimes impenetrable mountains.

He envisaged eighteen tunnels in twenty-eight miles of track
climbing down the Tehachapi Mountain to the San Joaquin Valley
below. The Southern Pacific Railroad was as merciless as it was
inventive. When a town denied access to the company,
it simply built another town.

The farmers too felt the brunt of the railroad's power.
Allowed to settle on isolated land, in Tehachapi, in Boron
and many desert regions of the state, many farmers had cultivated
the barren land into lush fields..

5.

In 1878, the Southern Pacific Railroad took titles to the land and
appraised the land at twenty-five to fifty dollars, instead of the two
dollars and fifty cents originally quoted the farmers.
Outraged, they went to court, where they lost every case.

By the end, eight farmers died and two hundred families were
evicted from their farms. Earlier, in 1881, the Southern Pacific
joined the Atchison, Topeka and Santa Fe Railway at Deming
in New Mexico territory to become the second transcontinental
          railroad.

My parents sang the song as we drove along, and so did we,
along with "I've Been Working on the Railroad," "Give Me a Ticket
for an Airplane," wanting, I suppose now that I think of it,
to be anywhere but the car.

For all their invention and cruelty, the founders of the railroad
obviously had a vision of shared beauty built into their machine.
The dining cars of the early railroads were elegant meeting places
where travelers met over fine china, eating roast pheasant, exotic

relishes and drinking California wine as they gamboled together
toward different destinations. The gilded age of the railroad ended
in 1910 when Hiram Johnson was elected governor of California
and methodically broke the political hold

of the Southern Pacific Railroad. A United States Senator
from 1917-1945, Johnson was the Progressive party's
nominee for vice president in 1912

6.

As a senator, he was an isolationist, opposing membership
to the League of Nations and the United Nations. A large state
on the edge of the Pacific, California itself is contained, isolated,
and like all things in isolation, it has no concept of boundaries.

Apotheosis of the "bedroom community," the suburbs
of Southern California are predicted in the next century
to reach Las Vegas. The Golden State, *El Dorado, California*
was the destination dream spot of millions of immigrants

from the 1800's when pioneers traveled the California–Oregon
trail, to the present day when Mexican émigrés are smuggled
across the border, camouflaged as part of the car's seat.

It can be no mistake that in the years during Johnson's
political career, the oil companies laid the foundation for
the state's eventual enslavement to the internal gasoline combustion engine.

With the downfall of the Southern Pacific Railroad,
the oil barons took, and continue to hold, the transportation
realities of the multitude of Californians who now inhabit

El Dorado, alone, or commuting, and mostly in traffic jams,
in automobiles along the state's freeways...

8.
My father died on July 21st, 2001, and on September 11th, 2001,
eleven boys in four airplanes crashed into the World Trade Center,
the Pentagon, and into a field in Pennsylvania,
killing themselves and thousands of people.

This has something to do with my father, with oil, with me.
My government and with you.

Since my father's death, I've slowly begun waking to my childhood.
It's mostly full of other people's words, as is time in general, the specific
a rare event, relying as it does upon an individual member being awake.

I'm waking to my childhood in my own child's life,
the driving he loves on video games, a version of the driving I loved, asleep
in the backseat. May all his crashing be virtual.

In remembering is re-membering.
Heart and mind, body and soul, time and space, father and daughter,
we are separate; we are attached.

The mind knows this when the heart pulses freely,
dependent on its own muscle.
The soul itself is a muscle, both housed
and independent of its own body.

I'm aware of its contraction now, in the arc it's making outside me
as it follows the automobile's whine, which is a pulse too, surrounding
each moment of modern life.

Time is eternal in space. Trapped radio waves prove it,
as does my dead father's DNA wound through me.

Heaven, then, spirals in a dragonfly's hovering, look, just now,
and in its vanishing.

Same Dream

Each love loved
Taps away at the already
Loved. So I have
Tried to love my first
Self and so she has
Fled me. So I have
Loved only you, Ben,
Until what we became
Opened, and let Lucie in.

from *O, Heart* 2015

Primary Directive

The woman is alone on stage

She is next to a tree

Then on top of the water, a huge dress floating

Yes, the woman is alone with herself on stage

She is looking toward something we cannot see,
You cannot see, watching her

It is her life, and it is there, in sequence, in a slide
Show, before her eyes behind

Her eyes—We cannot see

First, there was a dollhouse, it was not hers

Second, the two thumbs her own and oh, so soon,

A figure that loves her who is standing over her talking

The woman looks reflective, amused even,
And her hands move like speech

First Acts

The woman is alone on the stage

"His eye would trouble me no more . . ."

What was in Poe's heart
That all his tales express the outward
Murder or death of something—

Old men, eyes, Ligeia, hearts, etc—
While the narrator goes quickly crazy himself,
Embodied and disembodied, in the act?

"Meantime the hellish tattoo of the heart increased . . ."

And no one can tell if it's his
Or the old man's, though it becomes clear—
Nothing becomes clear.

In the 19th century,
People believed that emotions
Came from the heart
But now we know
That they come from the brain—
Emotions, and that helps us to—

Ahab and his whale,
Hawthorne and "The Birthmark"
And *The Scarlet Letter,*
All these signs signifying

The Red Badge of Courage

Every girl loves a coward

Edna swimming out to sea
At the end of *The Awakening,*
Swimming away from possession,
Swimming into the possession
Of her own heart,
Which drowns her

Scene 4, Act 2

"Occitania alone produced women troubadours
. . . the women's language is in every sense, new. . ."

Her heart is a violin
Loving her stranger

It is the shape of a flame,
A tongue and it reaches—

The violin loves her,
It is a shape,
A whole shape:
It is pity

Stop it

The violin loves her
It is a shape,
It is a tongue,
It is a movement toward

Are you looking at her?
Can you see what is in her eyes?

She is alone,
Holding a violin,
Cradling a violin
In the bend of her elbow

It is crying,
She is crying,
And feeding it
From her mouth

A clearing opens up around them
There is a sound
A sound   it is peace

Some worry and some more

She is bending and bowing
Bending and bowing
And the violin's notes
Turn upward turn away
And through the clearing,
Their clearing, the woman
And the sound she is making

They are so happy,
Going nowhere,
They are so happy,
Leaning into nowhere.
Please never let it stop—
Please never let it stop—
Please never let it—
This sound this movement moving

Second Acts

She is standing alone on the stage
And the empty space conspires with her

Emptiness conspiring with the various
Strains the violin threads through
—her heart?

"Now we are come to the cold time
When the ice and snow and the mud
And the birds' beaks are mute
(For not one inclines to sing);
And the hedge-branches are dry—
No leaf nor bud sprouts up,
Nor cries the nightingale
Whose song awakens me in May."

She is looking out past you
She is seeing a woman
She thinks is herself
Alone at a desk

She sees her often
Sitting at a desk
Sitting at a desk by a window
There are trees
It is dark

She wonders if she has ever
Really seen her
The woman she thinks is herself
Sitting at a desk with windows and trees

If she cannot be sure she has seen her
The woman desk-window-trees
If she cannot be sure
This sight is sight
Then why should you want
Her questionable picture?

The woman is a sound,
A movement toward a conclusion.
A present and visible memory
Of a sound and a shape, that seems true to her.

Voice-Over

Because I am going to die
I wonder at the models

Killing others to find
You've ended your own life

Swimming solo with your own heart
Until you can't keep going anymore?

Emily Dickinson begs the question

As does Emily Brontë
Really all of the Brontë sisters

And Hawthorne's really large heart
In Hester Prynne, her loyalty
To an absent minister,
Her devotion to invisibility,
Her charity

Zenobia is Hester outed,
A visible model of progressive womanhood
And her submission to Hollingsworth's
Utopian ideals make her trivial,
As is anyone in search
Of a consensual answer

The woman's heart keeps rising
To something she can't see

Cast

O, HEART: A DRAMA, BOTH "CLOSET" AND VERSE

SHE: SOMETIMES KNOWN AS "THE WOMAN"

HE: REFERED TO AS "THE STRANGER'"

THE HEART: THE ORGAN AND THE ENTITY, "THE KING" AS PERCEIVED VIA STRUCTURES HISTORICAL, SCIENTIFIC, MUSICAL, LITERARY AND OTHERS

THE EYE: WHAT IT SEES, WHAT IT CAN'T, HOW IT FAILS OR SUCCEEDS IN REVEALING _____

LYRIC: SELF-REFERENTALITY, A PRETTY SONG DYING IN ITS OWN CHORDS

CORDELIA: A SPEECH AND A FIGURE TOWARD HEART'S END

THE EAR: ITS VIRTUE, ITS AVAILABILITY AND INABILITY TO KEEP OUT, OR DISCRIMINATE

JANE BOWLES: SISTER TROPE

WILLIAM HARVEY: FATHER HEART

HESTER PRYNNE: ANGEL TROPE

HYSTERIA: THE TRUTH AVAILABLE IN HER, NOT TO BE CONFUSED WITH "SHE" OR "THE WOMAN"

POE: ANTITHETICAL MAN OR THE AUTHOR'S

AVERSION TO THE BAROQUE

KATE CHOPIN: TROPE OF RESCUE

EMILY DICKINSON: SOLO TROPE

EMILY BRONTË: ANTITHETICAL WOMAN OR THE AUTHOR'S AVERSION TO THE LITERATURE OF OBSESSION

PITY: A CHRISTIAN IMPULSE, A SORROW, A MANNEQUIN

Scene 5

*Any listening room in the world. Pity is there, reading The Scarlet
Letter aloud to Jane Bowles and The Woman, who are drinking,
who have been drinking, for hours. There are books all over the
room, some open facedown, all with paper clips serving as
bookmarks. The Stranger looks through the window, flanked by
William Harvey, stethoscope on The Stranger's heart, looking
puzzled. Lyric poetry circles in a ticker tape over the borders of the
room, which they read in fits and starts, shouting, like brokers on
the floor of the stock market.*

Pity: "The child could not be made amenable to rules. In giving
her existence, a great law had been broken; and the result was a
being whose elements were perhaps beautiful and brilliant, but
all in disorder; or with an order peculiar to themselves, amidst
which the point of variety and arrangement was difficult or
impossible to be discovered."

Jane Bowles (*after a deep drink*): My own baby girl. Or me.

The Woman: No, just Pearl. Who could be most any, free, little
girl. Yet still, a character in a novel, the nemesis of Beauty, that
culture diva, and thus a new form whose direction is forward
(*stops, pointing to the ticker tape, begins to recite, laughing so hard
her drink comes out her nose*):
>   When as in silks my Julia goes,
>   Then, then (me thinks) how sweetly flowes
>   That liquefaction of her clothes . . .

Pity: I hate you two! (*throwing the Hawthorne novel on the floor
she stomps out of the room*)

The Woman: You would! Who needs a Pity party anyway?

Jane Bowles: (*picking up the book Pity has left behind, reads*):
"Throughout all, however, there was a trait of passion, a certain
depth of hue, which she never lost; and if, in any of her changes,
she had grown fainter or paler, she would have ceased to be
herself,—it would have been no longer Pearl!"

The Woman: Li-que-fac-tion. Let it flow!

Outside, *William Harvey bangs on the window, but the women don't*
hear him, only a slight beating they think are moths against the pane.
He uses his stethoscope like a microphone and reads from his treatise
on the circulation of the blood, the De Motu Cordis.

Harvey: "The right and left sides of the heart work together,
causing blood to flow continuously to the heart, lungs, and body."

Jane Bowles (*hand to her heart*): My sister!

Harvey (*reading*): "It is helpful to visualize the heart as two
separate pumps,

Working in series—Right heart pump, left heart pump.

The heart has four chambers,

Two are muscular chambers that propel blood.

Two hold the blood

Returning to the heart and at just the right moment, empty."

Jane Bowles (*looking into her empty glass, nodding, shouts*): Empty!

Pity (*returning grumpily*): I know you think I'm done, but you
need me.

(Jane Bowles and The Woman speak, almost at once):

Jane Bowles: I wrote you, and replaced you with love.

The Woman: I became you and died.
(*Enter Emily Dickinson*)

Emily Dickinson: I heard a fly buzz – when I died – You two really need to get a room.

The Woman (*reading from the ticker tape*): I celebrate myself, and sing myself / and what I assume, you shall assume.

Jane Bowles: Jeez.

William Harvey: Apocrypha!

Emily Dickinson: And you wonder why I never left home!

The Woman (*reading from the ticker tape*):
> I'm learning to hold myself
> The way I wanted you, or anyone
> To hold me, and see, I don't even need
> A mannequin to break my fall.
> I'm authentic
> I break my heart all by myself.

William Harvey: Interesting. I wonder if it's true.

Jane Bowles: It's true.

Emily Dickinson: It's unimportant. This world is not conclusion.

William Harvey: Obviously.
(End of scene)

Mojave Letter

They had come to a crossroads,
No, they had come to a juncture,
A split place,

Where light was shining still,
Though they were not
In the sun, shining, or so it seemed, now

Though the sun
Had been omnipresent,
They'd been under it for many years
& one day

She saw there was a weed, a long weed,
A mean and barbed thing
Poking from her side.
What a sad passage.

How had it come to be there, green
And twisted, low-lying and tenacious,
Stuck in her at an angle?

He, and she, we
The inconstant ones,
Though Auden's limestone was not their earth.

The issue in the split,
The issue in the juncture
And under the sun, with weed,

Was how to love there,
How to love now that
The beautiful boy had grown,

Auden's beautiful boy and ours.
Once I would have said the Christ child,
But our son bore no resemblance to that static star,
And I could see, could you?

The suffering boy who, almost grown,
Had come to know his resting place
Was not, as it had always been,

In his mother's arms. The boy glanced with side,
And then fully open, eyes at his father,
Who was gone now.

What is a man, what is a woman,
What are we now our Eros is wandering away,
Shuffling without form anymore
Save sympathy, save its body
In the shape of our son?

I stood beside, I touched
Her, she was a woman,
She loved us and she was calling our names.
She was older and tired,
But she was still standing
And she was calling us.

I must have lifted my eyes a dozen times,
Expecting you to come walking,
So fast as you do,
To appear suddenly at the corner,

Expecting again to lift
My eyes to meet yours,
Our story of us intact,

Pulling her, reaching through
Our Eros, to us.
I held her, waiting for you.

What can you tell me, poem,
About my stranger?

Is he safe,
Are they nice to him there,

Will you send him this weed,
The one I found growing in me,
This landscape
That is our whole life together?

Agape, The Woman Is Agape

There could be forgiveness,
If time can be forgiven
Its erasure of human importance

There could be forgiveness,
Or forgetting, which are rumored
To be the same thing

There could be forgiveness,
If forgiveness is a border
As the one I've experienced
Between the living and dead

My dead father shook my foot and I awoke
As I did as a child
And I was again a child

The pity of children is merciless
And in it all is forgiven
Tiny snail in the grass

My father had no hands to touch me
But he did

There could be forgiveness
If love is something invisible that crosses

Continuous Acts

O, heart
In which four different chambers
Help you live and die, continuously
The woman walks around
Chatting, eating—the book is fallen from her hand
She drinks in the beauty of her children's faces
As they change
She herself died
& yet they call her mother
She is now her stranger

Like the Roman baths that fell into decay
As soon as they were privatized,
The woman's period of possession
Is so many pages of antiquity
& Only those who love ruins
Love her
She is now her stranger

"It is helpful to visualize the heart as two separate pumps, working
                    in series—
Right heart pump, left heart pump. The heart has four chambers,
Two are muscular chambers that propel blood. Two hold the blood
Returning to the heart and at just the right moment, empty."

She is now her stranger, Grand Inquisitor of the different chambers
To help you live and die continuously.
Are we God or are we a book
Where is our body

Lucy the fossil, The Furies,
Catamite, Sheela na gig, Devi,
Synonymous with Shatki,
The Baubo, Artemis, Echo, Daphne,
Armless Venus d'Milo,
Heloise, Helen of Troy, Jeanne d'Arc,
God the Mother, The Gospel of
Mary, Mary the Mother of God,
The Rose of Sharon,
Rachel, The Shekinah

The recycled Beloved
Her heart turns to tragedy, turns away
Tragedy is a chamber where she dies continuously, living
The ruin moving through time

Our little girl draws hearts throughout my notebook,
The shapes irregular, elongated down the page,
Much like an actual human heart
Which is shaped more like an upside
Down pear than a valentine.
Her letters likewise do not recognize the constraints of space,
Nor know margins as she writes them from left to right
The stick people she draws
Are all the same size.
Perhaps they are the first God,
The mother-father, matro-pater,
Before they separated
And she was locked in a safe.
Your betrayal thus is historical, and inevitable.
Likewise (or thus inevitably) the woman
Has misplaced the God in herself
What is lost cannot be kind

The woman in time is always
Written out of the creation
This appears to be a function of economy
Or her participation in an economy
That is designed to reduce her
By the year 200, she has many times been excised from divinity
In 1977, the year I graduated from high school,
Pope Paul VI again declared
That a woman couldn't be a priest
Because "Our" Lord was a man

". . . Right heart pump, left heart pump . . .
And at just the right moment, empty."

Her spiritual exile is physical

During phase one,
The tube-like heart
Is much like a fish heart.
The second phase,
With two chambers,
Resembles a frog heart.
The three-chambered phase
Is similar to a snake or turtle heart.
The final four-chambered heart structure
Distinguishes the human heart.

Swim swim, hop hop, slither, and plod.
In the two beat something
Tangential and corrosive
Counter motions

I love my mother and while
My mother is not
Can not be said any longer to resemble a Lona Alice—
In sleep, in many moments—
She is my mother
Mine
Always contains
Not mine

The woman is not a ruin

"The creator, becoming arrogant in spirit, boasted himself over all
Exclaimed: 'I am father and God and above me there is no one.'
But his mother hearing him speak thus cried out against him
'Do not lie!'"

O, heart, our divinity
Generating, making itself grow,
Seeking itself, finding itself
Mother of, father of,
Sister of, itself,
Son and spouse,
Of itself.

Agape, The Woman Is Agape

But da Vinci is wrong.

At one and the same time,

In the same subject,

There are always at least two motions,

Desire and repentance, love and hate,

Staying home or leaving forever,

Staying home and leaving forever.

Music and silence,

The music in silence,

The silence in music,

The other of Christ,

The other of Hitler,

The women inside the woman,

The strangers inhabiting the man,

The rhythm of the heart,

At the closed center of your eye.

Notes

26. "The Majority" is the longest piece in *Essays Before a Sonata and Other Writings by Charles Ives* (New York: Norton and Norton Co., 1962), a collection written by the composer in the years 1919-20 where he confronts issues of private property and the necessity of limiting them. In it he asks the question: "Who are going to run things in the country—in this world, for that matter? A few millionaires, a few anarchists, a few capitalists, a few party-leaders, a few labor-leaders, a few political-leaders, a few 'hystericals,' a few conservatives, a few agitators, a few nice old ladies, a few self-sufficient reformers, a few holier-than-thou know it alls, or YOU!— the Majority—the people?"

In 2018, we can answer this question with a newer allegory: the 1%.

27. William Blake is reported to have said this in conversation with Mr. Robison.
In "History of Experimental Music in the United States," (John Cage. *Silence.*) Cage is promoting indeterminacy in music and the need for detachment. What is needed, he suggests, is attachment to "emptiness, to the silence…Why is this so necessary that sounds should be just sounds? There are many ways of saying why. One is this. In order that each sound may become the Buddha. If that is too Oriental an expression, take the Christian gnostic statement: 'Split the stick and there is Jesus.'"

28. A posy can be a small bunch of flowers, or a brief motto or inscription on a ring. In late Middle English it becomes a contraction of "poesy" from Old French *poesie*, via Latin from Greek *poēsis*, variant of *poiēsis* 'making, poetry,' from *poiein* 'create.' John Donne, among others, wrote posies. It also came to mean (of a person or their behavior) someone or something affected and attempting to impress others; pretentious.

41. This poem was written practicing "the outside" as developed by Jack Spicer in *The Vancouver Lectures*.

52. The first quote is from George Oppen's *Daybooks* and the second from *A Reader's Guide to the Social Sciences* edited by Jonathan Mitchie.

67 "Romanticism" is based on Picasso's 1905 "Mother and Child."

81. "Armistice" collages the words from Homer's *Odyssey*, quotes from Simone Weil's notebooks when working in the Renault factory during World War 2, and an abbreviated list of murder-suicides reported in the *Rocky Mountain News* in 1992.

88. "Word" is a speech improvisation of Rodney King's 1992 appeal for calm after a bystander's film of his beating by LA police failed to stop the acquittal of four of the officers, which led to the 1992 Los Angeles riots. His whole statement: "People, I just want to say, you know, can we all get along? Can we get along? Can we stop making it, making it horrible for the older people and the kids? ... It's just not right. It's not right. It's not, it's not going to change anything. We'll, we'll get our justice ... Please, we can get along here. We all can get along. I mean, we're all stuck here for a while. Let's try to work it out. Let's try to beat it. Let's try to beat it. Let's try to work it out."

86. *Ave Verum Corpus*, or "Hail, True Body," is a poem composed to Mozart's requiem by the same name.

93. "And Its Discontents" mediates the categories of "inside" and "outside" which Freud defines in his theory of the subconscious, while quoting from his essay on the struggle between the individual and the civilization which he discusses in "Civilization and its Discontents."

101-112. Quoted passages in "Bluff City" are freely adapted from the writings of Martin Luther King Jr., Sigmund Freud, and Louise L. Hay's self-help book *Heal Your Body*.

113. "Gravity and Grace" is a song constructed from words from Simone Weil's text by the same name.

118-119. Words in "Oar" and "Embers" are in part constructed from the writings of Mahatma Gandhi.

153. "What is Meant Here by the People" plays with lines borrowed from Francois Lyotard's book *La Condition Postmoderne: Rapport sur le savoir (The Postmodern Condition: A Report on Knowledge)*.

156-164. "Everybody's Autobiography" freely adapts information from the Southern Pacific Railroad's official website and memorials to its history at the Museum of the Southern Pacific Railroad in Sacramento, California.

175-213. Passages in "O, Heart" are freely adapted from Edgar Allen Poe's "The Telltale Heart," Nathaniel Hawthorne's *The Scarlet Letter*, the poems of Emily Dickinson, Jane Bowle's *My Sister's Hand in Mine*, and Sir William Harvey's treatise on the heart *De Motu Cordis*.

Acknowledgments

Thanks to Cleveland State University Press, The University of Georgia Press, Alice James Books, and New Issues Press for permission to reprint selections from my earlier books here. Grateful acknowledgment is made to the following journals and anthologies in which the poems from *We Step into the Sea* first appeared, sometimes in different versions:

Barrow Street: "Life-Sentence(s)"

Cab/Net: "Nutshell"

Devouring the Green: "Little Elegy for Bill Knott"

Electronic Poetry Review: "Oboe Hymnal" (as "To Adam"), "After a Lifetime Spent in Air," "Outside Story"

New American Writing: "Permanently Stranger," "Poem with Some Word from Charles Ives' 'The Majority,' The Ghost of ee cummings Presiding"

The Cincinnati Review: "Her Name Was Rape," "The Sorrows of Separation Were Shifted," "What is God Is in Us."

The Literary Review: "In the Primer of Primary Things," "Segundo Primer" (as "In the Primer of Sorrowful Things")

Volt: "In the Primer of Material Things" (as "So One Just Keeps Going") "Getting Particular," "The Power and the Glory"

Barrow Street Press, the editors, and the author would like to thank and acknowledge all of the affiliated people and presses for permission to reprint the poems from past collections, as follows:

Refinery. Copyright © 1994 by Claudia Keelan.
   Reprinted with permission of Cleveland State University Press.
The Secularist. Copyright © 1997 by Claudia Keelan.
   Reprinted with permission of University of Georgia Press.

from *Refinery* (Cleveland State University Press, 1994)
"No Excuses"
"Sanctuary"
"Romanticism"
"Where the Train Meets the River"
"Refinery"
"Lines Where the Fence is Crossed"

from *The Secularist* (University of Georgia Press, 1997)
"The Secularist"
"Something to Keep"
"Armistice"
"Demography"
"The End Is an Animal"
"*Ave Verum Corpus*"
"3. Word (from "Beloved")"
"Parable 2"
"Parable 5"
"And Its Discontents"

from *Utopic* (Alice James Books, 2000)
"Toccata with Child"
"Bluff City"
"Gravity & Grace"
"Blue Diamond"
"Oar"
"Embers"
"Debts: Before the Afterward"

from *The Devotion Field* (Alice James Books, 2004)
"Critical Essay"
"The Scarlet Letter"
"*Via Negativa*"
"Poetry Anthology"
"T'is of Thee"
"Hello Beloved"
"Southern Anthology"
"You Are My Sunshine, My Only"
"Summer Anthology (Ives)"
"Instead of Reading Marcus Aurelius"

from *Missing Her* (New Issues Press, 2011)
"Came Capsizing the Human Boat"
"Pity Boat"
"Mary Wasn't Sure"
"Little Elegy (American Justice)"
"What is Meant Here by the People"
"About Suffering They Were"
"Everybody's Autobiography"
"Same Dream"

from *O, Heart* (Barrow Street Press, 2015)
"Primary Directive"
"First Acts"
"Scene 4, Act 2"
"Second Acts"
"Voice-Over"
"Cast"
"Scene 5"
"Mojave Letter"
"Agape, the Woman is Agape"
"Continuous Acts"
"Agape. The Woman is Agape"

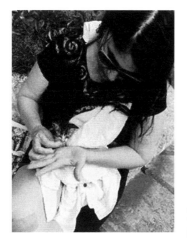**Claudia Keelan** was born in Southern California when it was still covered with orange groves, and NATO began the embargo, still in place, against lovely Cuba. Her teaching career has spanned all corners of the US, as she's taught in many writing programs, including the University of Iowa Writers' Workshop, the University of Alabama, where she held the Coal Royalty Chair in Poetry, Boston College, Rhodes College and the University of Nevada, where she is a Barrick Distinguished Scholar. Her honors include the Beatrice Hawley Award from Alice James Books and the Jerome Shestack prize from the American Poetry Review. The author of eight additional books, Keelan is a poet, literary scholar, and translator, who lives in the Mojave Desert with the poet Donald Revell, son Ben, daughter Lucie, standard poodle Miss Margaret Jarvis, and a worried schnauzer named Dugan.

BARROW STREET POETRY

We Step into the Sea: New and Selected Poems
Claudia Keelan (2018)

Luminous Debris: New & Selected Legerdemain
Timothy Liu (2018)

Whiskey, X-Ray, Yankee
Dara-Lyn Shrager (2018)

For the Fire from the Straw
Heidi Lynn Nilsson (2017)

Alma Almanac
Sarah Ann Winn (2017)

A Dangling House
Maeve Kinkead (2017)

Noon until Night
Richard Hoffman (2017)

Kingdom Come Radio Show
Joni Wallace (2016)

InWhich I Play the Runaway
Rochelle Hurt (2016)

Detainee
Miguel Murphy (2016)

The Dear Remote Nearness of You
Danielle Legros George (2016)

Our Emotions Get Carried Away Beyond Us
Danielle Cadena Deulen (2015)

Radioland
LesleyWheeler (2015)

Tributary
Kevin McLellan (2015)

Horse Medicine
Doug Anderson (2015)

This Version of Earth
Soraya Shalforoosh (2014)

Unions
Alfred Corn (2014)

O, Heart
Claudia Keelan (2014)

Last Psalm at Sea Level
Meg Day (2014)

Vestigial
Page Hill Starzinger (2013)

You Have to Laugh: New + Selected Poems
Mairéad Byrne (2013)

Wreck Me
Sally Ball (2013)

Blight, Blight, Blight, Ray of Hope
Frank Montesonti (2012)

Self-evident
Scott Hightower (2012)

Emblem
Richard Hoffman (2011)

Mechanical Fireflies
Doug Ramspeck (2011)

Warranty in Zulu
Matthew Gavin Frank (2010)

Heterotopia
LesleyWheeler (2010)

This Noisy Egg
NicoleWalker (2010)

Black Leapt In
Chris Forhan (2009)

Boy with Flowers
Ely Shipley (2008)

Gold Star Road
Richard Hoffman (2007)

Hidden Sequel
Stan Sanvel Rubin (2006)

Annus Mirabilis
Sally Ball (2005)

A Hat on the Bed
Christine Scanlon (2004)

Hiatus
Evelyn Reilly (2004)

3.14159+
Lois Hirshkowitz (2004)

Selah
Joshua Corey (2003)